"With his usual wit and command of language, Alex Parker fingers fifty of South Africa's greatest oxygen thieves… A thoroughly enjoyable read… Very funny"

– David Bullard, NewsTime

"They're all here, neatly skewered and steeped in scorn. Brilliant"

– Andrew Donaldson

"Entertaining and enlightening [with] well-researched descriptions that contain some very clever humour but also some very harsh criticism… Leads to many belly laughs and it comes highly recommended"

– Business Day

"Despite its subject matter, *50 People Who Stuffed Up South Africa* is just as much fun to read as it must have been to write – largely because of Parker's pithy and often humorous style"

– The Daily Maverick

"The writing is sharp and the scope impressive… *50 People Who Stuffed Up South Africa* provides some great moral sword fights and it's worth reading for the cartoons alone"

– Rapport

"Parker manages to balance cynicism and optimism, and his blend of sardonic humour and scathing social commentary make for a surprisingly relaxed read"

– The Big Issue

"Although the concept is an inherently depressing one, Parker's lightness of touch means one ends up laughing more often than crying at the cast of characters that people his book"

– The Witness

"Alex Parker is an equal-opportunity offender. From Jan van Riebeeck to Julius Malema… [you'll] find little argument here with his pick of those we love to hate"

– The Times

50 PEOPLE WHO STUFFED UP SOUTH AFRICA

Alexander Parker
with cartoons by
Zapiro

Published by Two Dogs
an imprint of Burnet Media

•

Burnet Media is the publisher of Mercury and Two Dogs books
PO Box 53557, Kenilworth, 7745
South Africa

info@burnetmedia.co.za
www.burnetmedia.co.za

•

First published 2010, reprinted 2010, 2011 (six times) and 2012
9

•

Publication © 2010 Burnet Media
Text © 2010 Alexander Parker
Illustrations © Zapiro

•

•

Distributed by Jacana Media www.jacana.co.za

•

Printed and bound by Ultra Litho, Johannesburg

•

ISBN 9781920137335

Burnet Media | MERCURY TWO DOGS

About the author

Alexander Parker is a freelance journalist and author whose work has appeared regularly in a variety of South African newspapers and magazines, including the *Sunday Times, Business Day, The Times, The Weekender, Wanted, Stuff Magazine, The Witness, The Financial Mail, Personal Finance, FHM* and *Top Car*. He is the author of *25 Cars To Drive Before You Die*, and was the producer of four, and presenter of two, seasons of SABC3's *Car Quest*. Alex believes that history is full of people who went on to make history because they didn't know their history. He tries not to be one of them.

About the illustrator

Zapiro – also known as Jonathan Shapiro – is the editorial cartoonist for the *Mail & Guardian*, the *Sunday Times* and *The Times*. Born in Cape Town, he studied architecture and became active in the UDF in 1983. He was detained by the security police shortly before taking up a Fulbright Scholarship at the School of Visual Arts in New York in 1988. He has published 14 cartoon collections, the most recent of which is *Do You Know Who I Am?*, as well as a large-format hardcover, *The Mandela Files*. He has received numerous international and South African awards and holds two honorary doctorates.

Acknowledgments

This book could never have been written were it not for the support and advice of some brilliant people. My parents, Jim and Jeannie, were the first to badger me into seeking a publisher. As time wore on and the list grew, the assembled masses of South Africa's motoring journalists, especially Hannes Oosthuizen, Pierre Steyn and Jesse Adams, assailed me with suggestions and ideas. I shamelessly mined the rich vein of knowledge that runs through the huge brain of 702's Stephen Grootes, and am grateful to the *Sunday Times*'s Stephan Hofstätter too, and to the Mullins clan down Durban way. Thanks, too, to my various editors – Gary Cotterell, Annaleigh Vallie, Katy Chance, Daniel Browde, Monique Tyrer, Toni Muir and especially Toby Shapshak – for their support during this fascinating, but time-consuming, process. A special thanks to my editor, Tim Richman, who is grossly over-endowed with literary talent and who hammered this thing into shape. My interest in South African history was kindled by David Rattray, who for some reason – pity, perhaps – took me in and let me work with him on the battlefields. Without him it wouldn't have even occurred to me that history was anything other than a collection of dates. Thanks, too, to Nicky Rattray, who lets me come and visit Rorke's Drift from time to time. A big thank you, of course, goes to Zapiro for supporting this project with his genius cartoons; and to his assistant, Eleanora, for all her help. And last, but far from least, to my wife Aneshree, who puts up with me swearing at the television, and my daughter Olweyn, who seems to have forgiven my extended hours in the study. They are the centre of my world.

To Olweyn

Contents

13	Randall Abrahams
14	Coleman Andrews
18	Wouter Basson
22	Richie Benaud
25	The bitter expat
27	Sepp Blatter
32	PW Botha
37	Lord Carnarvon
39	Bheki Cele
43	Leonard Chuene
47	Hansie Cronje
51	Eugene de Kock
55	Dingane
58	Alec Erwin
64	Bartle Frere
68	The guy I sat next to at the polo
71	Steve Hofmeyr
74	Sol Kerzner
78	Lord Kitchener
82	Louis Luyt
86	DF Malan
90	Julius Malema
94	Ananias Mathe
98	Khanyi Mbau
100	Thabo Mbeki

106	Lord Milner
109	The minibus taxi driver
112	Joe Modise
116	Patrice Motsepe
118	Robert Mugabe
122	Essop Pahad
124	Kevin Pietersen
128	Andries Pretorius
130	Cecil John Rhodes
136	Jackie Selebi
140	Schabir Shaik
145	Shaka
150	Stella Sigcau
154	Rudolf Straeuli
159	Mike Sutcliffe
161	Eugène Terre'Blanche
166	Mark Thatcher
170	Andries Treurnicht
174	Manto Tshabalala-Msimang
179	Jan van Riebeeck
183	Marthinus van Schalkwyk
186	Hendrik Verwoerd
193	BJ Vorster
196	Snuki Zikalala
200	Jacob Zuma

Introduction

I AM NOT SURE OF THE DATE, but at a guess it would have been 1999 or thereabouts. I was in London at the Royal Geographical Society (RGS) to attend a lecture given by my friend and mentor David Rattray on the Anglo-Zulu War of 1879. I was particularly excited because David had told me that none other than the legendary Sir Wilfred Thesiger would be attending. At a reception after the lecture, which had captivated a packed RGS, I was sort of nervously hanging around, until David, typically, told me to stop lurking about like a fool and introduced me to the world's greatest living explorer, then about 80 years old.

I forget what I said, but I do recall shaking his hand. David always used to say that "history is not that old", and back then, shaking the hand of the grandson of Lord Chelmsford (he of Isandlwana infamy), I certainly felt its proximity.

David used to tell a wonderful story about Thesiger. On his last trip to South Africa, Thesiger visited Isandlwana on the anniversary of the battle, the 22nd of January. There were the usual goings-on – folk dressed up as redcoats, an impi, political bigwigs, various ceremonies and prayers and so forth. And then there was this old, bent man with his weather-beaten face and alert, sharp eyes. One cannot imagine what it was like for Thesiger to visit the place that would have had such monumental significance in his family. All we can do is remark on how this old English gentleman reacted to it.

The way David used to tell the story, IFP leader Mangosuthu Buthelezi, whose own grandfather had fought at Isandlwana, was also attending the ceremonies. Thesiger spotted Buthelezi and approached him, whereupon these two dignified old men – one an icon representing British colonialism, the other a Zulu chief – held each other in a long, tearful embrace, something the local news photographers managed to miss.

I think there would have been no better image of reconciliation, and no better story with which to illustrate the extraordinary nature of this country.

The names that follow in this book are a decidedly mixed bunch. They count among them the egotistical, the incompetent and the corrupt. Some caused death and misery and mayhem. Some created the problems we still face today. Some can be considered "great" in certain ways, and yet are deeply flawed. Some are pure evil, some profoundly silly. Some threw it all away and some never had it. Some are just annoying, and some represent many of the names that didn't make it onto the list. But all of them, together, stand as a slightly odd monument to the people of this astonishing country.

Inevitably, the compilation of a list of notorious South Africans will be cause for some debate, perhaps even anger. You may disagree with the inclusion of certain individuals in these pages, or indeed the omission of others. Please feel free to voice your opinions to the publisher via email: info@twodogs.co.za.

Lastly, a word on the title of this book. I hope it's not too controversial – or, rather, that it's just controversial enough. Because as much as I've enjoyed delving into the sordid tales of some of the dodgiest and most destructive people to have taken their toll on our country, I can't say that I agree with the premise. It's just that *50 People Who Tried Their Damndest To Stuff Up South Africa But Couldn't Quite Manage It In The End* isn't as catchy, is it? So, while the various and varied characters featuring on these pages may have done their best to stuff up this fine land in which we live, I must declare their collective failure. It's why I choose to live here. I love the place.

Alexander Parker
November 2010

Randall Abrahams

b. 26 July 1969

Media specialist; radio and TV personality; nasty judge
on reality shows; nasty guy in real life

SURE, HE'S A SELF-IMPORTANT, UNLIKABLE, unfriendly turd sandwich who just loves the sound of his own voice, but he gave us *Idols*, goes the defence. Oh no, you've got it wrong, defence. He's a self-important, unlikable, unfriendly turd sandwich who just loves the sound of his own voice, *and* he gave us *Idols*.

Moving swiftly on to the real troublemakers...

Coleman Andrews

b. 1954

*US businessman; CEO of SAA (1998-2001); recipient
of a golden handshake representing the zenith of South
African parastatal wastefulness and mismanagement*

IN LIFE CERTAIN THINGS ARE TO BE EXPECTED. Death and taxes, of course. But there
are other simple notions that all right-thinking people would agree upon, such
as the notion of reward for work, and increased reward for especially successful
work. Work hard, get things right, and if all is well with the universe you will be
appropriately compensated. Such is the fundamental nature of this common sense
that this is generally how things go. That is, of course, unless you're head of a South
African parastatal. Then things get positively paranormal.

You see, things are different at our state enterprises. Having a monopoly means
you can change the rules. What's a client to do, for example, if Transnet decides to
rename itself Choo-choos R Us and charge for services in French francs. Switch
over to another operator? Oh, wait…

In essence, this means parastatal CEOs can do no wrong. It is a physical
impossibility for them to cock up, because they are the only players in town – and,
besides, the shareholder (the state of South Africa) has a bottomless pit of capital
(South Africa's taxpayers) to bail you out when the shit hits the fan. So go ahead,
boys! Do your worst! Make us gasp! Dazzle us with your breathtaking ineptitude!

In 2005 the boss of Denel, Victor Moche, was fired by Alec Erwin. For his
sterling efforts he received a R3-million golden handshake.

In 2007 the Land Bank paid out R4.5 million to Alan Mukoki when he quit as
CEO despite reports of fraud amounting to R2 billion.

In 2009 the SABC was forced to pay ex-CEO Dali Mpofu R11 million after an
embarrassingly managed period of political infighting. *(See Snuki Zikalala.)*

In February 2010 Jacob Maroga, who was CEO of Eskom during the calamitous
2008 rolling blackouts that are estimated to have cost the country $50 billion in
direct losses, was given a R2.3-million performance bonus, despite – get this –
having been fired the previous year for poor performance. By the time of his
departure he was on an annual salary of R5 million, not including bonuses. Well,

presiding over the destruction of wealth and prosperity in South Africa was, we have to admit, a particularly creative effort. To add a further dose of madness to the affair, Maroga has subsequently sued Eskom for R85 million in "reasonable damages" as a result of his dismissal. *(See box.)* He seems to have a valid case.

But these indefensible, sense-defying examples of sheer wastefulness are really loose change when compared to the efforts of South African Airways to insult and abuse the country's tax-paying citizens.

"Former Eskom boss Jacob Maroga has slapped the embattled parastatal with a massive R85-million lawsuit. In a civil claim filed at the High Court in Johannesburg, the ousted Eskom CEO demands "reasonable damages" unless he is reinstated to the position he left under a cloud at the end of last year...

Maroga, whose five-year contract had been due to expire in 2012, is demanding everything he was entitled to had he not been given the boot.

This includes R14.5 million for loss of salary, R45 million for incentives and R7 million for other benefits.

His claim shows Eskom paid:
• R1 million a year for a "dedicated protector and driver" for Maroga, and a driver for his family;
• R500,000 a year for security at his Kyalami Estates, Midrand home and R100,000 for general home support;
• R1 million a year for "personal assistance";
• Just under R100,000 a year for a petrol and garage card and insurance for his Mercedes-Benz C350; and
• R5,000 a month for medical aid, up to the age of 80.

The papers reveal how, at just over R5 million, Maroga's annual salary was twice that of president Jacob Zuma and three times that of [then Minister of Public Enterprises Barbara] Hogan."

– Times Live news report, 23 January 2010

Remember Khaya Ngqula, head of SAA until 2009? He was fired as CEO of our national carrier as a result of a R1-billion tender-rigging saga, among other accusations of fraudulent mismanagement. Now, of course, this was considered a jolly good show in parastatal-land, so he was given an R8.9-million payout as a pat on the back. His predecessor, André Viljoen, no doubt would have been dismayed to hear of Ngqula's annual R5-million package; his was around half that, though he made up for it with multimillion-rand performance payouts which, in 2004, totalled around R4.5 million – this for a CEO who, in his last two years at the top, presided over losses of more than R15 billion.

But the best of them all, the absolute corker, was a particular individual by the name of Coleman Andrews, who was shipped in from America in 1998 to turn around the ailing national carrier and appeared to be doing exactly that. He received excellent annual performance reviews and was rewarded with simply ludicrous bonuses: some R110 million in three years, according to sources. So far, so capitalist. Then, just like that, SAA decided that they didn't like what he was doing and that he had to go. And the punch line? With no grounds whatsoever to fire him, they had to pay him out – to the tune of a further R98 million. Which meant that, after a three-year stint as CEO in which he was unable to realise his strategy for the company, Andrews ended up costing SAA R232 million.

To add insult to taxpayer injury, the CEO of SAA Technical, a Canadian by the name of Kevin Wilson, is alleged to have received R40 million shortly afterwards to also head off into the sunset, news that the public seemed to lose sight of at the time, possibly because of the R232-million mushroom cloud obscuring their view. Or maybe, by then, it was just a coping method.

Because such is the way of the modern South African parastatal. Sound management is fleeting at best, accountability nonexistent; wastefulness abounds and politics is king – and together they are ruinous.

There is, however, a glimmer of light at the end of the tunnel because SAA appears to have realised that rewarding staff members for potentially criminal incompetence isn't exactly "best practice". Ngqula was eventually made to pay back his golden handshake and was sued for R30-million compensation for his wasteful expenditure. Finally, SAA appears to have made the correlation between remunerating employees with vast amounts of money in exchange for shoddy or pointless work and the dire straits in which the company exists.

But the darkness at the end of that light is that these figures – even Andrews's obscene R232 million – pale in significance when compared with, and are simply representative of, the billions and billions of rands that are being squandered annually on the parastatals themselves through similar mismanagement. And, assuming you're a decent citizen, that money is coming straight out of your pocket.

Wouter Basson

b. 6 July 1950

*Former head of South Africa's chemical-and-biological-
warfare project; public embodiment of apartheid state's
amoral race-superiority mentality; "Dr Death"*

HE'S GOT THOSE EYES. They don't look at you as much as see through you. If you've encountered him in the flesh you will have felt that creepy shiver they impart down your spine. And if there was ever a smile – and we suspect that in the course of his work there probably was – it would never reach those soulless eyes. Because Wouter Basson was and is, if his reputation is anything to go by, a truly nasty piece of work.

Basson's claim to fame is as head of Project Coast, a project so benignly named that it could only ever have been born of sheer evil. It was apartheid South Africa's biological-and-chemical-warfare operation, and it was established during PW Botha's disastrous reign as the deep paranoia and flourishing bunker mentality of apartheid's endgame set in. *(See PW Botha.)* Those in charge of countering the communist onslaught were worried about the possibility that Cuban and Angolan troops, and not to forget Swapo, were eventually going to end up with chemical and biological weapons (CBWs) and use them on South African troops. As the twisted logic with these things goes, the solution to this apparent inevitability was for South Africa to develop a CBW programme of its own, work on which began in the late 1970s. It was, at least initially, intended to be defensive.

But, of course, under Botha things were to change. The decision was made to ramp up the project and incorporate it into the apartheid regime's offensive arsenal for combatting the state's enemies. And that meant they would need a man untroubled by the idea of using such weapons against civilians and political activists to run the show.

Turns out the president himself knew such a guy. God knows what they used to chat about during their appointments but, unbelievably, Botha just called up his personal physician, a cardiologist called Basson. And Basson went about his new work with the kind of destructive vigour that waters the eyes.

Now, it so happens that Wouter Basson has not been convicted of anything.

He appeared before the Truth and Reconciliation Commission, but dismissed the opportunity to reveal the secrets of the apartheid state's CBW programme in return for amnesty. Instead he was charged in 1999 with 67 counts of murder, conspiracy to murder, drug offences and fraud, of which he was acquitted after an exceptionally expensive two-and-a-half-year trial, despite the testimony of nearly 200 witnesses. The judge, much criticised afterwards, ruled that several important charges for crimes committed outside of South Africa could not be prosecuted and refused the admittance of vital evidence.

> "Basson's scientists were working with anthrax, cholera, salmonella, botulinum, thallium, E coli, ricin, organophosphates, necrotizing fasciitis, hepatitis A, and HIV, as well as nerve gases (Sarin, VX) and the Ebola, Marburg, and Rift Valley hemorrhagic-fever viruses. They were producing crude toxins (and some strange delivery systems) for use by the military and police, and they were genetically engineering extremely dangerous new organisms – creating, that is, biological weapons."
>
> – *Extract from a profile on Basson titled "The Poison Keeper" in The New Yorker, January 2001*

There were ugly scenes at the courtroom, with former defence minister Magnus Malan and General Constant Viljoen present. They seemed satisfied with the result. One of those who found Basson's lack of contrition less pleasing was Frank Chikane, who had survived an assassination attempt by apartheid agents in 1989, when his clothes were laced with poison allegedly supplied by Project Coast. "For me the issue is not whether or not somebody gets found guilty," he remarked. "The real issue is whether or not the person is able to come to me and say, 'I did this and am very sorry'."

There was, it seems, never much chance of Basson doing that (though former Minister of Law and Order Adriaan Vlok publicly apologised to Chikane in 2006). In his time on the stand, Basson testified that he had free reign to do pretty much as he pleased as head of Project Coast and that he had learnt much of his trade from Saddam Hussein's regime, but that he'd never done anything illegal, really.

So, for the purposes of the remainder of this entry, we will have to rely on unproven allegations against Basson and Project Coast, mostly from the TRC testimonies of their alleged victims. There are, to the country's shame, reams of these testimonies, and they make for diabolically horrific reading. A selection of the project's activities runs like the plot to some kind of twisted splatter movie.

Project Coast was required, naturally, to act against apartheid enemies who were, naturally, mainly black. That's why it sought to create "smart" poisons that would only affect black people. It also hoarded enough cholera and anthrax to start epidemics, and plans were made to disperse them into black townships via water supplies and other means.

Small-beer ANC activists and the like were tied to trees and smeared with poisonous gel, then left overnight to see whether the gel had killed them. If not, a lethal injection of muscle relaxants would finish off the job. Bodies of activists – some dead, some simply sedated – were dropped into the sea from light aircraft.

Project Coast really wanted to perfect that art of killing. Other ideas included sugar laced with salmonella, cigarettes infused with anthrax, chocolates poisoned with botulism and whisky-and-herbicide cocktails. Everyday objects were modified to deliver a lethal dose of poison, for example umbrellas and walking sticks that fired pellets, syringes disguised as screwdrivers, and poisoned beer cans. There was even, it has been claimed, a plot to poison Nelson Mandela's medication with thallium, a toxic heavy metal, prior to his release from prison. The inventiveness was astounding, and seems to indicate a particularly disturbing relish for the job by those in the programme.

Project Coast also went in for mad, non-lethal stuff, including ecstasy grenades for crowd control. It was this use of "recreational" drugs in his work that eventually caught up with Basson. In 1997 he was arrested for selling a huge amount of the rave drug to a police officer in a sting operation. Some say it was a stitch-up because the ANC government was (understandably) keen to nail him for anything it could, while others say "Basson's brownies" are sorely missed on the rave scene. Either way, police found three trunks of material related to Project Coast at his house, evidence that eventually led to his trial. The material was supposed to have been destroyed, but wasn't – which made observers wonder just how much dirt Basson still has, and on whom exactly. Botha, his other apartheid bosses, US intelligence agencies? Since then there have been allegations that Basson has sold his expertise to Iraq, Iran and Libya.

The sad fact about Wouter Basson is that we may never know the full extent of the activities of this man, and he may well live the rest of his life as a free citizen, unlike his apartheid-jackboot counterpart Eugene de Kock. *(See Eugene de Kock.)* Only a case by the Health Sciences Research Council still hangs over his head, and if his last trial was anything to go by he won't be too concerned.

Basson, in his role as head of Project Coast, came to personify to a tee the sickness that was apartheid, the horror of it, the illness that allows men to do to other men what he is alleged to have done. Many of apartheid's criminals feature in these pages. They all had something of Wouter Basson about them.

Richie Benaud

b. 6 October 1930

Australian cricket captain (1958-1964); internationally acclaimed commentator; reason for the South African cricket team's "choker" tag

LET'S BE STRAIGHT UP ABOUT THIS: Richie Benaud is an absolute legend. Never has a globally respected authority on cricket combined such a gentlemanly and unassuming knowledge of the game with such a sartorially smashing collection of off-white sports jackets. Whether it's beige, cream, ivory, light tan, vanilla, bone, bamboo, sand, camel or cashew, Richie wears those jackets like a king, and in doing so he must rank as one of the most loved and lovable names in all of sport. And an Aussie at that.

But the man right royally screwed us over. And by "us" I mean every cricket-loving South African who's ever yearned for the sweet taste of World Cup victory.

Casual observers of the recent history of South Africa will often point to that fateful World Cup semifinal in Birmingham in 1999, when Lance Klusener took us to the brink of a sensational victory over Australia before it was tragically snatched from under our noses by a needless run-out, as the moment when we assumed the mantle of crunch-match chokers. The game ended in a tie, with the Australians progressing to the final on a superior run rate, and it's no understatement to suggest that the psychological damage inflicted on South African fans that day cast a pall of gloom over the country for months, possibly years, to follow. Even today, the memory still raises a tremble of moisture in the eye.

But our failure in key knock-out matches goes back further than that – to 22 March 1992 to be precise. The venue was the Sydney Cricket Ground and the match was another World Cup semifinal, this time against England. Back then, we were the new kids on the World Cup block, having recently returned to the international fold after years in the sporting wilderness, and no-one fancied our chances going in to the tournament. But we'd played out of our boots and somehow made our way to the semi on the back of a tight bowling attack, Peter Kirsten's artful bat and Jonty Rhodes's inspirational fielding.

The game was a cracker, hanging in the balance from start to finish. Donald got Gooch early, and Pringle bowled well, but the Zimbabwe-born Graeme Hick hit a fluid 83 before a late flurry from Reeve got England to 252 in 45 overs. South Africa hadn't bowled the full 50 overs by the designated end-of-innings time, so the tournament rules – and here's where Richie starts getting involved, because he's the man credited with devising them – necessitated that the five overs not bowled be simply lobbed off both the English and South African innings. An odd rule, many would have concluded at the time, but not as odd – or cruel – as that which governed the target re-calculation after a rain delay…

South Africa started the chase at a good clip, with Hudson hitting 46 off 52, but we lost wickets regularly and were struggling to keep up with the required rate by the middle overs. Rhodes then got the chase back on track with a typically livewire 43, before he, too, lost his wicket, and it was left to stalwarts Brian McMillan and Dave Richardson to take us through the last critical overs. Then, with 22 required for victory off 13 balls and McMillan on strike, it started to rain. Not too heavily, mind you, just enough to get the players off the field. For 12 minutes. Twelve fateful minutes.

> "This game's closing minutes buried South Africa's World Cup hopes, and whatever credibility the rain rule had retained… The losers were disconsolate, the winners embarrassed, and the crowd furious. Why, they asked, were the two overs not played out under the floodlights?"
> – *Review of South Africa v England*
> *1992 World Cup semifinal, Wisden Almanack 1993*

Once again, Richie's rules kicked in, and when play resumed South African fans were aghast to see that our allotment of overs had been reduced by one while our target remained steadfast: 22 required off 7 balls, read the SCG scoreboard. Suddenly, a tricky situation had transmogrified into a Herculean task – a near-miracle was required, all because of a ridiculous formula that saw the runs scored in the least expensive over of the English innings, in this case a Pringle maiden, being deducted from the target. Meanwhile, the weather was now fine and the floodlights were blazing – there was all night to finish the game. But the farce was not yet complete: somewhere in the ground the minute hand on the relevant timepiece ticked over once more and it was deemed that yet another over had been lost, this time in conjunction with one run from the target: 21 runs were required off just 1 ball*. Now, not even a miracle would suffice. A stone-faced McMillan

---

* The TV display and scoreboard incorrectly indicated 22 runs required.

prodded the last ball of the match away for a single, and we'd lost by 19 runs. A potentially brilliant climax had been reduced to absurdity; South Africa's unlikely World Cup dream was over.

"Twelve minutes of rain was all it took to wreck a classic contest and produce the sort of farce that so often crops up when cricket's regulations get themselves in a tangle," wrote Cricinfo's UK editor Andrew Miller, when reviewing the match some years after the fact. But those 12 minutes didn't just wreck a classic match. In the years and competitions to come, it seemed that those 12 minutes had instilled in South African cricket the notion that, come the critical moment in a high-profile knock-out match, the fates would conspire against us. First it was the bizarre rain ruling in Sydney; then it was one-man-team Brian Lara destroying us in the 1996 quarterfinal in Karachi (again by 19 runs); then that tragic run-out in Birmingham in 1999; then another debacle in the rain in 2003, this time against Sri Lanka in Durban, when poor Shaun Pollock and Eric Simons couldn't get their maths right… By the 2007 World Cup the team, now ingrained with angst-filled bewonderment at our inability to pull off the big victory that our world rankings suggested was our due, tried to just relax and not get expectations up – a strategy that saw us limp into the semifinals, only to be rolled over by Australia like the blind school's 5th XI.

So, after more than a decade as one of the top two ranked ODI sides in the world, what do we have to show for our endeavours? Well, we did win the inaugural ICC Champions Trophy in 1998 in Bangladesh – and that's it. Amazingly, we haven't even made it into a World Cup final yet. Not one.

How is this possible? Why does it happen?

No-one can say. But we've got to blame someone, and in the absence of any other contenders, it has to be Richie. Marvellous!

The bitter expat

Internet-surfing prophet of South African doom; secret yearner for "the next Zimbabwe"; global PR disaster

No-one's got a problem with people who choose to emigrate. We really do now live in a global village. Freedom of choice and freedom of movement are (practically) universal rights, and the trade in human skills, or simply the expression of human preference, means that millions of people cross borders every year in search of a better, happier, more satisfying existence. Sometimes they get it, sometimes they don't. Either way, it is considered normal behaviour.

In South Africa, though, the emigration issue is fraught with angst and bewilderment. Given that we can't even pick a sports team in this country, or attend a job interview for that matter, without a seemingly irrelevant politically motivated distraction to consider, perhaps this is just the way it's got to be. But wouldn't it be nice if it wasn't? Wouldn't it be that much more pleasant going to bed at night knowing that there weren't scores of bitter and twisted expats out there trolling internet forums, posting comments on South African news sites and generally belittling the country of their birth from abroad?

It really shouldn't be this way. Just think of the hundreds of thousands of emigrants who have disappeared across the waters, often to our great loss, and who haven't looked back. Or who look back regularly, and even visit regularly, but when they do it's with joy and magnanimity in their hearts. They love and miss South Africa – it's just that they've found a more satisfying, more lucrative and/or more love-filled life in another country, like so many other migrants around the world.

There's a good explanation for this vocal minority of disaffected Saffers living abroad, and it boils down to insecurity. They've made the effort, they've paid the money, they've uprooted their lives and, because they're not really satisfied where they are, they now need to justify their actions. A bit like bumping into your saucy ex down at the pub and then spending the rest of the night explaining to your mates why you broke up with her. Essentially, it's therapy – though, it must be said, not particularly effective therapy. (In fairness, the nearly-as-vexing corollary phenomenon exists, too: the defensive stayer, who refuses to countenance any news or opinion on South Africa that is not considered 100-percent positive.)

"As opposed to the quiet expat who just heads off overseas and gets on with his new life – and good luck to him – the bitter expat loves nothing more than painting his adopted land as a modern Utopia while prophesying the imminent social and economic implosion of the country he's left behind. The sinking ship, the dying beast, the next Zimbabwe. Oh, it's coming. Just around the corner. Promise. Never mind that the UK's a bit wet or New Zealand's a touch average or Australia's full of Australians or Canada's a wee bit boring – those of us foolish enough to stay behind are all destined to be murdered in our beds, for sure.

The doom mongers have been proselytising for years now, ever since the end of apartheid loomed on the horizon in the '70s and '80s. Mandela freed, 1994 elections, Mandela retired, rand through the floor, ANC with a two-thirds majority… With every historical landmark the fire and brimstone becomes that much more imminent, and yet somehow, amazingly, astoundingly – infuriatingly! – South Africa has not yet fallen apart at the seams. Even when JZ finally wormed his way into power, the surest sign yet that we were about to tip into the sea, nothing really changed.

In fact, not that much has changed in the past 30 years. We still get by, we still bitch about the idiots in charge, we still have a jol – which is particularly galling for the bitter expat out there living in First World mediocrity, because even though he secretly yearns for home a part of him wants South Africa to fall apart, to justify schlepping across the world to Brisbane or Vancouver or Galway or wherever the hell he finds himself. Whether it happens now or later is neither here nor there. Because in 2187, when South Africa does finally come apart at the seams, when inflation maxes out at a gazillion percent and the cryogenically frozen Julius Malema returns to install himself as dictator for life, there he'll sit croaking with glee into his oxygen-replacement vat… "See? See? Told you so!"

– *Extract from Complete Kak! by Tim Richman and Grant Schreiber*

So, one asks, how has the bitter expat stuffed up South Africa? Surely, his departure is good riddance? Well, yes and no. Yes because that's one less bore at the braai to deal with, going on about "they" and "them" and the good old days. But no because these people are becoming our modern representatives to the rest of the world; cliquey narrow-minded Saffers happy to do a hatchet job on the country they've left behind. It's just not good marketing.

And besides, you can avoid those braais if you want – or at least you can call the individual in question on his comments, if the mood happens to take you. But the internet is a platform for sheer, unadulterated madness. And sometimes you just want to read the news or the sports or Thought Leader in peace.

Sepp Blatter

b. 10 March 1936

President of Fifa; controversy-surrounded dictator of
world soccer; modern coloniser of South Africa

"THEY COULD, FOR EXAMPLE, HAVE TIGHTER SHORTS. Female players are pretty, if you excuse me for saying so, and they already have some different rules to men – such as playing with a lighter ball. That decision was taken to create a more female aesthetic, so why not do it in fashion?"

Ah, yes, that drunk lout down at the pub, you might imagine. A gormless chauvinist man-comment between friends, perhaps? Nudge nudge, wink wink, know what I'm saying?

But no. This was the considered opinion, as expressed into a microphone, of the most powerful person in the world's biggest sport. This was president of the Fédération Internationale de Football Association Joseph Blatter's solution to expanding the popularity of women's soccer – and he wasn't even kidding. "Let the women play in more feminine clothes like they do in volleyball," he declared to avoid any ambiguity.

This, then, is how Sepp Blatter sees women's soccer – as a highly attractive collection of 22 lovely pert buttocks and 44 lovely pert breasts jiggling about like excited puppies on a soccer field for the amusement of… well, he probably hadn't got that far. He probably just thought it'd be fun for Sepp Blatter. Because, mostly, whatever Sepp Blatter wants, he gets. Certainly, when there are dollar signs involved, he is most persuasive.

So, then, this was the same man who was going to bring the Soccer World Cup to Africa. The same man who has, in his dictatorially long 12 years at the helm of Fifa, veritably swum in controversy brought on by foolish comments, churlish behaviour or various and varied allegations of corruption. What were, we wondered, his Friday-night pub musings about little old South Africa?

Well, after the Germans stole our World Cup bid in 2006, he had decided, like a creepy uncle, to bestow upon Africa that most sacred of rights: the right to be colonised by a viciously ruthless money-making machine called Fifa.

Now, look. The 2010 Soccer World Cup – excuse us, the 2010 FIFA World Cup™

– it is pretty much agreed, went extremely well for South Africa. It revealed to the world a side to our country that doesn't tend to get reported too much in, for example, the British tabloid press. All that stuff about how beautiful it is here and how wonderful the average South African is and how awesome our weather is and how good our roads are and how OR Tambo International is streets ahead of most European airports and how brilliant our hotels are and how the beer is pretty good but the wine is out of this world. You know, the *good* stuff – the reasons we all choose to live here despite the people inhabiting these pages.

> "Fifa cannot sit by and see greed rule the football world. Nor shall we."
> *– Sepp Blatter, commenting on billionaire club owners in October 2005*

So, it's important to separate the positive nature of the World Cup from the appalling behaviour of the organisation that owns it. Because the Cup also went well for Fifa – to the tune of something like $3.2-billion in turnover. Which works out to an estimated $2-billion profit, a truly phenomenal figure. And it made this enormous amount of money by treating South Africa like some kind of colony, a country it bought with the promise of colourful beads and shiny bangles in order that it might plant its flag in our soil, plunder what it wants and jauntily disappear off the next morning with its swagbag over the shoulder.

The FifaMafia came to town with Don Blatter in the lead, and roughed up our government into creating an environment where only Fifa and its large international partners were able to really profit from the event. So that's great for a company like Hyundai, but not so great for Average Johannes who owns a B&B in Cape Town. Fifa was exempted from paying income tax, VAT, import duties and levies on the import and export of goods. In all, South Africa probably lost hundreds of millions of rands in potential revenue in order to allow Blatter to bring his till to South Africa. All the while, Fifa's restraint-of-trade clauses were draconian and absolute; small-business owners were regularly hauled off to court for the slightest violations; informal traders were hounded from making a living in most of the major cities; and in the run-up to the event, South Africans were, at times, made to feel like strangers in their own country.

On top of those ignominies we also forked out something in the region of R63 billion for upgrades to stadiums and various infrastructural developments, necessary parts of the deal for us to secure Uncle Sepp's special Christmas present. And here's where it really starts to bite – because, by comparison, that's actually pretty much what the arms deal finally cost us.

In the end we did well. The stadiums looked amazing, the years of frustrating roadworks worked out in the end, and some of what we're left with has been a categorical success. You cannot argue with the magnificence of Durban's Moses Mabhida stadium, and the fact that it seems to be working financially too. (Touch wood.) Soccer City in Soweto has also been brilliant, with a bright future as the country's premium soccer, and even rugby, venue.

The Cape Town Stadium, on the other hand, is the archetypal multibillion-rand white elephant, which it was, most annoyingly, predicted it would be from the very moment it was mooted. Everyone – literally every soul in Cape Town who follows sport – always knew this was going to be a costly mistake, that there were at least two far more viable venues, that after the tournament it would sit there, empty and unused, like a great big monument to Blatter's vanity – and yet it went ahead anyway.

It went ahead because Sepp Blatter didn't like the massively cheaper alternative: an upgrade to Athlone Stadium, in the heart of Cape Town's soccer-mad community. Too many poor people's houses ruining the view. And what of Newlands Rugby Stadium, then, a perfectly suitable venue that hosts hundreds of thousands of spectators at major rugby and soccer matches every year? Nope, Blatter wanted a better shot of Table Mountain, stuff the cost and the consequences. Which, to no-one's surprise, came in at nearly four times the initial budget – reportedly R4.4 billion at the end of it all. That there is real talk about flattening Cape Town Stadium as the cheapest way to manage it is terrifying to contemplate.

This particular example proved just how much our smarmy benefactor really cared about South Africans. But there were other examples too: the outrageous attempt to foist a R50,000 fee on any establishment daring to show the soccer on the television while it sold alcohol, comes to mind, and the fascist decrees of what may be eaten, drunk and worn in any one of "Fifa's" stadiums.

When confronted with these unpleasant facts, Blatter's top henchman, Jerome Valke, insisted that Fifa's massive profits were "to protect football" and that "80 percent of Africa would have no soccer" were it not for the organisation. But here's the ugly truth: Fifa spends more money on operational expenses in the average year – around $800 million – than it does on football development around the world. Its headquarters, opened in 2006, alone cost $200 million to build.

Blatter himself has made grand claims in the past about aiding "the entire African continent". How on earth he believes he's aiding Africa by dropping an unneeded multibillion-rand stadium on Cape Town is, in the final analysis, more than tricky to discern. The figures simply give the lie to his haughty claims. Blatter and co are no better than the colonists of old, flattering to deceive with supposed improvements to our country as they run off with the loot.

South Africa may have benefited in many ways because of the World Cup, but not at all because of Blatter and his Fifa conquistadors. In reality, they stole from all of us, and benefited us little. What good came out of the World Cup was down to us, and us alone.

"God helps those who help themselves," Blatter opined in a press conference in June 2010, in a less-than-subtle intimation that South Africa shouldn't be looking to Fifa for much post-World Cup assistance. But you could see where he was coming from – it's worked well enough for him.

PW Botha

12 January 1916 – 31 October 2006

Premier of South Africa (1978-1989); Border War advocate; apartheid icon; Rubicon non-crosser

HIS FATHER WAS A BOER WAR *BITTEREINDER* and his mother was locked up in one of Lord Kitchener's concentration camps. He grew up on a horse farm in the Free State and inherited a bullying, aggressive demeanour along with a powerful sense of Anglophobia and general racism – and he was destined to lead South Africa through its darkest days.

Pieter Willem Botha had the opportunity to claim greatness. It was right there on a platter in front of him. Instead, in the face of an ever more appalled world and increased international pressure, he retreated into his laager, bitterly defending it and everything he had done to protect it to the end. There was, for many, something almost comical about *Die Groot Krokodil* by the end of it all. The silly nickname, the wagging finger, the awful temper, the laughable inability to accept he'd been wrong… One particular quote of his (echoing a similar sentiment from Hendrik Verwoerd made years before) seemed to epitomise this vision of Botha: "I am sick and tired of the hollow parrot-cry of 'apartheid!' I've said many times that the word 'apartheid' means good neighbourliness."

Of course it did, Mr Large Crocodile.

But, really, there's nothing funny about PW Botha's achievements. The man took a discredited ideology and instead of saving this nation from it, he allowed it to define the past 30 years, and God knows how many more to come.

Botha was a politician all his adult life; he even left university before graduating to get involved in Cape politics. Like all good Afrikaner nationalists of his era, he had a grounding in the pro-Nazi Ossewabrandwag, which he joined as the war against Hitler approached. He was, however, savvy enough to renounce their socialist leanings with the Allied victory near, and he hopped aboard DF Malan's Christian-nationalism bandwagon instead.

Botha's rise up the political ladder was solid, if unspectacular. After ten years in parliament as representative for George, he was made deputy minister of internal affairs by Hendrik Verwoerd. Then came the crucial post of defence minister in

1966 under BJ Vorster. And when Vorster quit in 1978, Botha was elected prime minister. He'd made it to the top.

Let us not get distracted by talk of Botha as a reformer. He was at the core of apartheid. This is what he had to say about the separation of the races, the heart of apartness, in 1964: "I am one of those who believe that there is no permanent home for even a section of the Bantu in the white area of South Africa and the destiny of South Africa depends on this essential point. If the principle of permanent residence for the black man in the area of the white is accepted then it is the beginning of the end of civilisation as we know it in this country."

Botha, it is true, did open negotiations with the ANC, on a small, hush-hush level. He legalised interracial relationships and marriages. For some, the evidence of his more liberal approach to the black people of South Africa came with his introduction of pathetic scraps of suffrage for Indians and Coloureds – but there was never mention of black representation, which he could never countenance.

As defence minister, Botha was integrally involved in the management of the South African Border War from its first engagements in 1966. He presented apartheid South Africa internationally as the only weapon against the spread of communism in Africa, and the South West Africa-Angola border was his critical front. Over the course of the following 23 years, the terrible and vicious campaign in support of Jonas Savimbi's Unita was waged by young men who had been forced into the strict two-year draft, also one of Botha's babies. While his direct involvement in an essentially unwinnable war – sometimes referred to as "South Africa's Vietnam" – has always been a secondary charge on Botha's rap sheet of leadership offences, the scar left on a generation of South Africans is a deeply enduring one.

In the 1970s Botha presided over South Africa's nuclear programme, eventually ensuring that the state was armed with six nuclear bombs. The man was in his laager, but now, instead of the muzzle-loaders of Andries Pretorius's day, the boerevolk had nukes. Somehow fate averted the use of our very own A-bombs – and just how close we got we'll never know – but Botha's reign and influence still had a long way to run and should not be overlooked.

In 1983 he pushed through a new constitution, abolishing the position of prime minister and investing those powers in a state president – namely himself. By then he was rolling. Under his rule, South Africa meddled in civil wars in Angola and Mozambique, wars that utterly ruined both countries; the SADF sent bombing raids into the so-called front-line states; there were South African-sponsored assassinations and attempted assassinations across Africa, with death squads even taking out various people in Europe; there were bomb attacks in Lesotho and Mozambique; and ANC members were regularly kidnapped and tortured.

Internally, police brutality was evident everywhere as the state cracked down on any "suspicious" behaviour. Those suspected of treason were hanged. The most trivial offence would result in a lashing – some say 40,000 blacks were whipped every year.

Of course, the madness could not endure forever. The international anti-apartheid movement, inevitable in the face of the increasing bloodshed in South Africa, started to have a serious impact on investment in South Africa. Large multinationals began pulling out; disinvestment hit hard. The pressure on Botha and his apartheid regime was coming to a head.

> "He must know Chris Hani is waiting there with a big fork and Steve Biko is waiting there with a big hammer."
> – *Nomamsi Diepu, speculating on Botha's reception in the afterlife, at his funeral in George, November 2006*

Botha was not an intellectual. As Frederick Van Zyl Slabbert described him, he "was extremely authoritative, militant and not very well read; he relied heavily on the people around him". Helen Suzman concurred, noting that he "was not enormously intelligent", but that "he had enough sense to realise that change would have to come because the black resistance was gearing up considerably and the opposition of the international community was growing very strong".

In 1985 he finally relented and met Nelson Mandela, later announcing that he would free the ANC man if he got the organisation to renounce violence. Mandela's response, read by his daughter Zindzi, was that under democracy there would be no violence, and that the apartheid state was its source. That same year Botha was scheduled to make a speech; a great deal was expected of it. It was, in his own words, time to "cross the Rubicon", and it was widely expected that Botha would announce wide-ranging reforms and perhaps even free Mandela and unban the ANC.

Sadly, *Die Groot Krokodil* was not up to it. Perhaps he lacked the courage; perhaps his intellect couldn't handle it. Botha kept the phrase "cross the Rubicon" in his speech, but removed the announcement of real reform that had followed it. He had missed his chance to be great, and South Africa was plunged into further violent chaos.

In 1986 a state of emergency was declared. The ANC made the townships ungovernable, complete with horrific necklacings for government collaborators. Sweeping, oppressive powers lay in the hands of the president, and Botha used them at will. Detention without trial was commonplace – by 1988 some 30,000 people had been locked up without trial. The media were censored; thousands were arrested, beaten and tortured.

These were the darkest of days, and Botha battled on stubbornly until even the Nats couldn't take it any more. After suffering a stroke in 1989, he resigned as leader of the National Party, assuming his nominee Barend du Plessis would take over. Instead, the party elected FW de Klerk. Botha was furious and refused to stand down as state president until he bitterly accepted a compromise with De Klerk.

To the end, Botha was impossibly stubborn and boneheaded. He fought the people of South Africa, the international community, and ultimately even the decisions of his own party. His downfall reportedly left him embittered throughout his final years. After democracy, he refused to attend Truth and Reconciliation Commission hearings, and he was convicted as a result. However, the ruling was overturned on a technicality. Botha crowed thus: "I will never ask for amnesty. Not now, not tomorrow, not after tomorrow."

Botha died in the comfort of his home at the age of 90. He never once appeared to suggest that there was any remorse for the mayhem he had forced onto the people of South Africa. As the *Mail & Guardian* editorial at the time noted, "One of the worst features of this arrogant and truculent man was his utter lack of contrition for the pointless suffering he caused so many innocent people. He could have tried to make his peace with them; he could have helped the truth commission heal the wounds he inflicted. Instead, he withdrew into a haughty sulk at his George home, on the state pension the ANC government continued to pay him."

There was surprising magnanimity when he died. The family was offered a state funeral, which they declined. President Mbeki lowered the flags at Tuynhuis in respect of a former president. We forget just how remarkable the ANC can be on occasions.

But I think that Cosatu probably represented the feelings of the average South African slightly more accurately with this comment: "He was the devil personified at the same level that Hitler was, and should be treated as a pariah by peace-loving people. It is fitting that both him and his time has come to an end. Good riddance."

Lord Carnarvon

24 June 1831 – 29 June 1890

Victorian politician; Secretary of State for the Colonies
(twice); architect of confederation of South Africa;
cause of mayhem, bloodshed and colonial resentment

HENRY HOWARD MOLYNEUX HERBERT, 4th Earl of Carnarvon, was known until 1849 as Lord Porchester, after which he succeeded his father in the earldom and assumed his title. But you can call him Twitters, which was his nickname back in the day. It seems appropriate, given that he was a cantankerous old fuddy-duddy who caused mayhem in South Africa.

Carnarvon was a senior Conservative Party politician during the glorious reign of Queen Victoria. He served in Lord Derby's cabinet as secretary of state for the colonies, but resigned in a huff in 1867 over Benjamin Disraeli's Reform Act, which doubled the number of eligible voters in Britain by enfranchising the English working classes. So you can guess which way he would have voted in South Africa's 1992 referendum had he been around.

A typical Victorian administrator, Carnarvon presided over the confederation of Canada with great success. Prior to his interventions, Canada had consisted of the Province of Canada (including Ontario and Quebec), New Brunswick and Nova Scotia. This was obviously wasteful and, fearing an aggressive United States to the south, Carnarvon considered it wise to confederate the provinces into the Dominion of Canada. That it worked is evident in the fact that the act itself, the British North America Act of 1867, remains the founding document of modern Canada. Believe it or not, Her Majesty Queen Elizabeth remains Canada's head of state. Carnarvon had been right.

Seven years after quitting cabinet, he deigned to return to his previous position, now under Disraeli, despite his distaste for expanded suffrage. He had enjoyed fiddling with Her Majesty's colonies before and felt he had some more fiddling in him. In surveying Victoria's dominions it occurred to him that what had worked so well in Canada was bound to work in South Africa. But this time he was wrong.

With little thought that the Boer republics might have another opinion, or that the pesky Zulus might not conform to his wizard little scheme, Carnarvon despatched various administrators to do his bidding, including Theophilus Shepstone and Bartle Frere, whom he appointed high commissioner and governor of the Cape – with disastrous consequences. The result was war, and lots of it.

The Ninth Xhosa War began in 1877 and the Anglo-Zulu War followed two years later. *(See Bartle Frere.)* Carnarvon's plans also led directly to the first British annexation of the Transvaal, in 1877. The annexation itself was notably bloodless. Shepstone, accompanied by just 25 troopers to act as his enforcers, rode up to Pretoria from Pietermaritzburg armed with a pin and a proclamation, which he then stuck to President Burgher's front door. Not a shot was fired. However, many of the sudden subjects of Her Majesty preferred things – once they'd had time to consider Paul Kruger's persuasive thoughts on the topic – the way they were. Resistance slowly mounted and the Boers eventually came to express their feelings

> "He [Carnarvon] thought it no harm to adopt this machinery [Canadian governing legislation] just as it stood, even down to the numbering and arrangement of the sections and sub-sections, and present it to the astonished South Africans as a god to go before them. It was as if your tailor should say, 'Here is a coat; I did not make it, but I stole it ready-made out of a railway cloak-room. I don't know whether you want a coat or not; but you will be kind enough to put this on, and fit yourself to it. If it should happen to be too long in the sleeves, or ridiculously short in the back, I may be able to shift a button a few inches, and I am at least unalterably determined that my name shall be stamped on the loop you hang it up by.'"
>
> – *Francis Reginald Statham, editor*
> *of the Natal Witness during the 1870s*

on their new-found citizenship in 1881 on the slopes of Majuba Hill, in what was to be the most prominent engagement of the First Anglo-Boer War. The battle saw nearly 300 British soldiers killed, captured or wounded, for just six Boer casualties. It was a humiliating defeat, which led to the signing of the Pretoria Convention later that year, acknowledging the Transvaal as an independent state.

Carnarvon's utterly lunatic scheme to force confederation upon a collection of people as cantankerous and warlike as those who inhabited southern Africa circa the mid-1870s was a madness that spoke of colossal arrogance and disregard for the suffering or wants of the people in question. With the sweep of his pen, he ignited bloodshed that ultimately laid the groundwork for the far more devastating Second Anglo-Boer War, which followed. *(See General Kitchener and Lord Milner.)*

Bheki Cele

b. 22 April 1952

National Commissioner of the SAPS; eternal VIP;
perfect example of politically appointed public servant
not realising he is, in fact, a public servant

BHEKI CELE IS AN IMPORTANT MAN. The problem is that it's not his genetics, his outfits, his money or his title that make him important. Cele is important because of the hugely intimidating scale of what it is he has to achieve. His job – to rein in the criminals and protect the rights of South African citizens – is what makes him important. But big Mr Cele can't seem to get past the fripperies and the benefits and the shenanigans. He seems to be sweating the small stuff. Perhaps the big stuff is too big, even for such a big man.

Let's start with titles. When he took up office in July 2009 as our national police commissioner he decided he couldn't function in the new role without a totally awesome form of address. So the first thing he did was make himself a general. National Police Commissioner General Bheki Cele – much better!

Let's be really clear about it. Mr Cele isn't a general because Mr Cele isn't a soldier. Policemen just aren't soldiers. Send soldiers to do a policeman's job and what you'll end up with is a lot more corpses than you already have. That's why you have an army on the one side to fight wars and kill people, and a police force on the other to fight crime and protect people. Cele may just as well have called himself Reverend Cele or Professor Cele.

And besides, Cele is a political appointment. He wasn't promoted within the police service and he has no previous professional crime-fighting experience. He hasn't had his "ass in the grass", as it were. So he has about as much moral claim to the title of General as Idi Amin had to being the King of Scotland. But our top policeman appears to suffer a similar case of elephantitis of the ego as that which afflicted old Idi, because in his own mind, it seems, Obergruppenführer Generalissimo Cele, Rear Admiral of the Good Ship Cop, *is* King.

Okay, look, if it makes him feel better, right?

Now, that whole crime problem. Let's get to work! But no, wait! Time for some dodgy thank-yous – for which we refer to the *Sunday Times* story of August 2010

about how Cele, too important to bother with tender procedures, rented a building for a cool half-billion of South Africa's finest tax rands. The article was headlined "Bheki Cele's R500m police rental deal" and it explained that there was nothing wrong with the building that the SAPS already used, it's just that the current cop shop was being leased from an Mbeki-aligned businessman. And the new one? You've guessed it – from a Zuma-aligned businessman.

"A billionaire businessman has clinched a dodgy R500-million property deal with police chief General Bheki Cele that will result in the police moving their headquarters to a building he bought this week.

The *Sunday Times* can reveal that Cele signed the deal to move SA Police Service top brass – including Minister of Police Nathi Mthethwa, his deputy, Fikile Mbalula, and administrative staff – to Roux Shabangu's building almost two months before he bought it.

The deal never went out to tender, violating Treasury regulations that all contracts over R500,000 must go through a competitive bid process. After three days of queries from the *Sunday Times*, the Department of Public Works could not explain why it had flouted Treasury rules."
– *Opening paragraphs of a Sunday Times report, 1 August 2010. Coauthor Mzilikazi wa Afrika was arrested three days later on an unrelated matter in what was widely considered a case of police intimidation.*

Good grief. Alright then, political favours returned – but we're used to that. Okay, so that crime thing, eh? Shall we?

No! Outrage and fury! Righteous indignation! A squad of policemen shuts down Biermann Avenue, Rosebank, home to Avusa Media and the newsrooms of *Business Day*, the *Sowetan*, *The Times* and, of course, the *Sunday Times*. Mzilikazi wa Afrika, coauthor of the story, is arrested by a threatening posse of Hawks representatives and hussled out of the building in front of colleagues. His house is raided, his phones, notebooks and laptops are confiscated, his car searched. Then he's driven to Mpumalanga where a bunch of Brigadiers and Colonels (the play-play kind, not the war-fighting kind) threaten him and ask him intimidating questions. Charges are brought, seemingly to do with a corruption story Wa Afrika has worked on but which never ran in the paper – and then they are very quickly dropped because there is absolutely no evidence he's done anything wrong, and because South Africans can't be locked up for being in possession of the truth (just yet, anyway).

Wa Afrika wasn't arrested – arguably kidnapped, seeing as he didn't have his rights read to him – because of the rental-deal report. Officially anyway. But the intimidation was there for all to see, and the parallels to the apartheid police state tactics of the 1980s were all too obvious.

Bheki Cele didn't come from nowhere. He fought in Angola and spent time on Robben Island. He's very loyal to Jacob Zuma. He likes jaunty hats and nice clothes and being seen on TV. For a while he was MEC for Transport in KwaZulu-Natal, where he was fond of being driven at extremely high speeds on the freeway – your classic blue-light muppet – and memorably defended such actions by very important politicians such as himself with that classic kneejerk get-out-of-jail card, by crying race. In one incident, a convoy was filmed travelling at speeds in excess of 160km/h, barging people off the road and whatnot, and the footage was given to local Pietermaritzburg newspaper *The Witness*. Cele's response to the citizen who had provided the evidence was this: "He is a self-made, arrogant, non-accountable individual who purports to be a good citizen and I will dare to argue that he is also a racist." Cele went on to attempt to bully *The Witness* into giving up its source which, to the paper's credit, it never did.

Indeed, bullying seems to be one of Cele's signature tactics because, evidently, the rules do not apply to His Worship. This is a great pity. It shows that Cele really believes all his self-hype, all the "General" bollocks. He actually, to his core, seems to believe he's a superior being when, in fact, he's a public servant and should be acting in the public's interest at all times. (Note to Bheki Cele: speeding dangerously when late for meetings is *not* in the public's interest.)

While many South Africans will have enjoyed Cele's tough talk on crime, in particular his requests that police "shoot to kill", the problem is that he's a redeployed cadre, utterly politicised and with no experience at fighting crime. On top of this, he appears to have no qualms in using the police as a private army to persecute those who displease him. And the concern is that the opposite may apply too: that the police is a private army that will not investigate those who *do* please the commissioner, or his political seniors.

To be fair to Cele, he only just scraped his way onto these pages. The ominous Wa Afrika fiasco clinched it. He hasn't done that much actively wrong just yet other than coming across as a self-important egomaniac straitjacketed by political loyalties. But the signs are there: his cadre deployment, the shoot-to-kill talk, the militarisation of the police service, the inability to prioritise and do some actual police work. He really does have looming disaster written all over him, and if Selebi was the frying pan then Cele is potentially the fire. *(See Jackie Selebi.)*

Dodgy top cops? We've been having it!

Leonard Chuene

b. 20 September 1952

Disgraced former ASA president; race-card user; the ugly face of politics in South African sport

THIS IS, SPECIFICALLY, A STORY ABOUT Leonard Chuene and Caster Semenya. Winnie Madikizela-Mandela features, as does the incomparable Julius Malema and a few others, and their details will fill the next 1,000 or so words. But it is, of course, an allegory. This is really a story about the continuing intrusion of politics into contemporary South African sport.

Didn't Leonard Chuene, former president of Athletics South Africa, make a consummate ass of us all? Rewind back to the 2009 World Athletics Championships in Berlin and think about the weeks that followed. Try to recall the feelings this guy, our top athletics administrator, engendered in you. Embarrassment? Horror? Sadness?

So, he had this superstar runner, a woman, who had shaved an impressive eight seconds off her 800m time in less than a year. He liked it when he heard that news. This would be great. Make old Chuene look good, you know. Especially after the debacle in Beijing.

But there was a problem. The woman in question was Caster Semenya, and questions were being asked of her gender. A sure-fire controversy was brewing. What to do, what to do…

Well, that shiny gold medal was beckoning, so Caster went and she ran and she won. No surprises at that result. And no surprises to anyone familiar with the case when it all started to unravel.

Word got out that the IAAF had requested Semenya undergo gender testing before the race, in Pretoria, and that they now wanted to conduct their own tests to prove that she didn't have an unfair advantage over other competitors. In admitting to the rumours, they breached Semenya's confidentiality and were rightly criticised for poorly managing the situation. The resulting media coverage was predictably frenzied and international.

And how did Chuene, our international representative, react? In the same way that any self-aggrandising incompetent South African official behaves when he's backed into a corner. To borrow from *The Onion*: "Quickly! Hide behind self-righteousness! Ready the *ad hominem* rejoinders! Dodge the issue at hand! Question its character and keep moving haphazardly from one flawed point to the next!"

Specifically, what Chuene did was cry Racism! Imperialism! How dare they! "This is about racism," he declared. "We are not going to allow Europeans to describe and defeat our children," he ranted. In a grandiloquent gesture of protestation against Semenya's treatment, he even resigned his seat on the IAAF board. And, of course, he out and out lied. No, he was not aware that the IAAF had expressed concerns before the event; no, he hadn't been informed of any test results before the event; no, he hadn't been advised to withdraw Semenya from the team...

> "According to a member of the medical panel, Chuene initially agreed to withdraw Semenya but changed his mind the following morning because he was worried what the reaction would be from politicians in South Africa if he 'withdrew a black South African woman who had a chance of winning gold.'"
> – *Sapa news report, 19 September 2009*

And then, as happens in South Africa when there's a race bandwagon in town, all the politicos jumped on board – the ANC, the ANC Women's League, the ANC Youth League, the Commission for Employment Equity – even president Zuma had (comparatively sensible) words to say.

The problem was that Chuene had created this mess all on his own. The IAAF was completely within its rights to run the tests – as they'd done to other athletes in the past – and race was, it goes without saying, never the issue. But Chuene *was* aware of the IAAF's position on Semenya, he *had* been informed of her initial test results and he *had* been advised by team doctor Harold Adams to withdraw her from the team before the athletes had even left South Africa. He had simply ignored this advice and sent a young, naive girl into the harsh and unforgiving spotlight of top-flight international sport and the media madhouse that accompanies it.

The team flew home and Semenya was met with a deeply embarrassing political carnival at OR Tambo. Winnie Madikizela-Mandela was there to greet her "granddaughter". Malema spread his special brand of divisiveness. Chuene mouthed off defensively once more. And Semenya sat quietly looking mortified. The *New York Times* described proceedings as "an event that seemed less a spontaneous burst of enthusiasm by sports fans than a choreographed welcome by political professionals". Or, as a local commentator put it, "the political muck-rakers emerged from their dark alleys and poisonous back rooms to hijack a cause and score some cheap points by fixating on a nonexistent racial issue".

By now, of course, it was out of control. The report on Semenya's gender had been leaked to an Australian website, which wrote that, while she has the external features of a woman, she has no ovaries; instead, she has internal testicles that are producing a lot of testosterone.

Meanwhile, the IAAF calmly tried to explain its position: that it had never sought to vilify Semenya and was merely seeking fairness in the sport. "Our legal advice is that, if she proves to have an advantage because of the male hormones, then it will be extremely difficult to strip the medal off her, since she has not cheated," a spokesman wrote to the AP. "She was naturally made that way, and she was entered in Berlin by her team and accepted by the IAAF." The IAAF ended the discussion with this: "After that, depending on the results, we will meet privately with the athlete to discuss further action." (Eventually, she was cleared to compete internationally again.)

Now, had Chuene not gone for the glory in the first place, had he looked at Semenya with a trace of humanity in his eyes, had he not ignored medical advice on the matter, then the delicate situation could have been handled entirely in private. Yes, Semenya would have missed an important event and South Africa would have won one less gold medal, but she would have ultimately retained her dignity and credibility in the face of life-changing medical news.

Instead we got a farcical circus, a deeply humiliated young woman and the rest of the world looking at South Africa and rolling its eyes. Racism? Hell no. There wasn't an ounce to be found. Just idiocy. Our idiocy.

Hansie Cronje

25 September 1969 – 1 June 2002

Cricketer; record-breaking captain of the Proteas; hero to children and adults alike; inspiration for aspiring players; lover of money; arch manipulator; liar; cheat; destroyer of dreams

IF EVER A MAN THREW IT ALL AWAY, it was Wessel Johannes "Hansie" Cronje. Born into a solid, middle-class Afrikaner family in Bloemfontein, Cronje was brought up among conservative Christian folk who lived for cricket and rugby, and he represented the Free State at school level in both sports. But his future was in cricket alone; he captained the SA Schools XI, and within a few years, at the age of 21, he was captaining his province.

Cronje was groomed for success and his timing couldn't have been better. To be an emerging talent in the late 1980s was to be at destiny's door. It was an exciting time in South Africa: the ANC was soon unbanned, Nelson Mandela was released and all of a sudden South Africa was playing one-day cricket in India. Cronje didn't get any game time on that particular tour, but he went along as one chosen for stardom. He was 22.

Indeed, Cronje would become a star brighter than even his auspicious beginnings might have suggested. His cricketing figures do not leap out of the page at you. In Tests he averaged around 36 with the bat and just under 30 with the ball; in ODIs it was around 39 and 34 respectively. These are good-quality all-rounder figures, especially in the abbreviated format, but they fall short of cricketing genius. Yet, as is often the case with averages in the gentleman's game, they don't tell half the story.

They don't tell you, for example, how brilliant Hansie was against spin bowling. He was renowned as the one South African who could savage Shane Warne at will, which he did on numerous occasions. Playing Sri Lanka at Centurion in 1998, he got down on one knee and hoiked none other than Muttiah Muralitharan for four, six, six and six off consecutive balls to take him to the (then) third-fastest Test fifty, off just 31 balls.

And while his bowling average is good as opposed to excellent, it too doesn't express quite how useful his medium pace was on the dead wickets of the subcontinent, and how tidily he could nail down an end to give the quicks a break. The figures also don't tell you how brilliantly athletic he was in the field, and how he, together with Jonty Rhodes and Bob Woolmer, revolutionised fielding preparation and fitness levels, changing the way cricketers approached the game.

And, of course, another thing the figures don't tell you is just how revered Cronje came to be, both by his own players and by South African and world fans.

By the time he became full-time captain of the Proteas at the age of 25, Cronje was already well regarded in the side. It was 1994. South Africa had a new, democratic government and a new, young cricket captain. For six successful years he led the South African team, growing in influence, popularity and importance to the game with every passing Test and ODI. The team was made up of clean, professional young men who kept on winning. In conservative South African circles they were genuinely adored.

As a leader, Cronje's record spoke volumes: he was in charge for 53 Tests, of which South Africa lost just eleven; and he won 99 out of the 138 ODIs he captained (with one heartbreaking tie in the 1999 World Cup semifinal).

Beyond these stats, though, Cronje seemed to get the best out of people, too. Woolmer, who coached the Cronje-era South Africans, spoke of his common touch: "His pre-match talks were often inspirational, and he led from the front." He was famous for making newcomers to the side feel at ease with his practical jokes, and for instilling confidence in nervous young men. Craig Matthews, for example, noted that Cronje "persuaded me that I was good enough to play international cricket".

Of course, all of this made the revelations that destroyed his career ever more shocking. Hansie Cronje had a weakness: "an unfortunate love of money", as he would so accurately put it. Some deeply unsavoury elements in India discovered this early on in his captaincy and proceeded not only to corrupt Cronje, but to ruin the reputation of the proud sport of cricket.

Cronje claimed to have rebuffed the first illicit approaches he received to throw games only two months after assuming the captaincy, against Pakistan in January 1995. A year later, though, Mohammad Azharuddin introduced him to the infamous MK Gupta on a tour of India. Later, Cronje fell into the clutches of one Sanjeev Chawla. There were others, too: bookmakers and match-fixers attracted to this powerful captain with unprecedented influence and that one fatal flaw.

Over the course of several years, Cronje accepted hundreds of thousands of dollars for sharing team information, game forecasts and his captaincy intentions. He underperformed in several matches, and tried on numerous occasions to lure team-mates into doing likewise. Various players, approached in groups or as individuals, turned him down over the years, assuming he was joking. He wasn't.

In a move that can only be judged – after a decade's review – as utterly and appallingly unconscionable, Cronje approached two of the most vulnerable players in his squad on a tour of India in 2000. Herschelle Gibbs and Henry Williams were insecure and naive youngsters who would do just about anything for their revered captain. He offered them, and they accepted, $15,000 each to play poorly in a One Day International. Meanwhile, Cronje told Chawla he needed $25,000 for each player, pocketing the difference. The plan went badly wrong, but Cronje's cupidity spoke loudly.

"I had great respect for Hansie Cronje. I thought, if he can do something like this, why can't I?"
– *Henry Williams, in his testimony to the King Commission*

"Fuck Hansie and all who sail with him... Hansie Cronje is an unscrupulous liar and the thief of far more than money. His greater iniquity is that he has stolen trust and faith from the young, that he has crudely eroded the happy optimisms of children."
– *Robert Kirby, from his Mail & Guardian column, April 2000*

According to his testimony at the subsequent King Commission, set up to investigate match-fixing in South African cricket, Cronje turned down approaches from bookies at regular intervals. But his love of money was "very similar to an alcohol problem", and he tumbled off the wagon in spectacular fashion, and perhaps most famously, against England at Johannesburg in 2000, when he contrived to manufacture a result in a dead-rubber Test against England. With the series in the bag and several days' play lost to rain, he persuaded England captain Nasser Hussein that each of them ought to forfeit an innings. It only emerged later that, prior to his magnanimous offer, Cronje had received a late-night visit from local bookmaker Marlon Aronstam and that as a result of his joint forfeit – which led to a South African loss – Cronje received R53,000 and a leather jacket as a gift for Bertha, his wife.

It was a phone call in 2000 between Chawla and Cronje that New Delhi police were listening in to that brought Cronje's edifice crumbling down. He initially denied the charges vehemently, and because of his irreproachable standing he was widely and equally vehemently supported by his fans. But the weight of evidence was altogether too much and, in a weepy late-night phone call to Ali Bacher,

Cronje confessed all.

The cricketing world was aghast, the damage huge. Literally millions of cricket lovers across the world saw their favourite sport revealed as a con, a lie, a broken dream. Cronje was but one of various big-name players involved – Azharuddin and Saleem Malik were two others – but the revelation of his disgrace was the most shocking because of the squeaky-clean Christian image he chose to convey.

Two years after "coming clean" at the King Commission, claiming that the devil made him do it, Cronje was dead, killed in an air accident near George. Today, the suspicions remain that he left countless secrets hidden or fudged and that the full extent of his cheating, lying and hypocrisy will never be known. There are at least 25 matches in which he was involved that remain under suspicion. And yet, as possibly the most profound testimony to the power of his personality, a great many South Africans cannot bring themselves to remember Cronje as anything other than a well-intentioned boy who took his eyes off Jesus. They conveniently forget that Cronje did his best to ruin a sport loved by millions, all for a few dollars and a leather jacket.

Cronje was an avaricious liar in a position of considerable influence. He sold out his country and made fools of his supporters for financial gain, he abused a hallowed position of power, he took criminal advantage of vulnerable team-mates who idolised him, and he cast a pall over cricket that has yet to dissipate – and, as evidenced by the recent Pakistani scandal, perhaps never will.

Outside of South Africa, where there is no Hansie neurosis, cricket fans regard his memory very, very poorly indeed. It wasn't the devil that made him do it. It was his unfathomable depths of greed.

Eugene de Kock

b. 29 January 1949

SAP colonel; Koevoet operative; Vlakplaas assassin;
bespectacled face of murderous apartheid brutality

IN ALL HONESTY, THERE ARE any number of people who could qualify for this spot. Most of them are faceless men who played the role of the steel toecap in the jackboot of the apartheid state. Consider, for example, overzealous soldiers in the Border War who committed appalling crimes of murder, rape and torture. Think about the small-town cops, or the border police, for whom there was no fallout for their physical brutality, be it for state purposes or simply for fun. And what of the state-security personnel who regularly encouraged prisoners to slip on the soap or try to jump to freedom from the tenth floor of John Vorster Square? The vast majority of these men have faced no court for what they did, and now they never will. But one man did, and that was because he was especially savage and efficient in his killing. He is serving a 212-year sentence for his conviction on 89 counts, six of which are for murder. His name is Eugene de Kock and, if you were affiliated to the ANC and you fell into his clutches, your prospects were bleak.

That's because, first of all, De Kock didn't kill just six people. The man who came to be known as "Prime Evil" performed his most famous work as the commander of Vlakplaas, a South African Police counterinsurgency unit, but he had been schooled in another counterinsurgency outfit, Koevoet, which operated against Swapo in what was then South-West Africa, and had thousands of "terrorist" kills credited to it.

Koevoet operators were notoriously skilled at tracking guerillas and it was a hugely respected and successful fighting unit. But they were also notoriously savage and cruel. A casual browse of the archives of their deeds from the Truth and Reconciliation Commission makes for appalling reading. Arbitrary murder was common. Torture more so. Koevoet deliberately cultivated a reputation to be feared. Tricks like tying captured enemy – sometimes dead, sometimes alive – to the fronts of their Casspirs and then driving them through the bush, acacia thorns and all, ensured as much.

This was how De Kock learnt his trade, and, in the face of worsening agitation

in the townships in the 1980s, he was called back from the horrors of the bush war to apply his skills on the civilian population of South Africa. He would do so as the leader of Vlakplaas, essentially a government-sponsored hit squad named for the farm that served as the unit's headquarters.

As its founder and commander, De Kock was given free rein to do as he saw fit to crack down on the ANC-led insurgency. He took this to mean – and later declared that his superiors did, too – capturing those working against the state, torturing them and then attempting to turn them into spies. If that failed, he murdered them.

For those who would never be turned, Vlakplaas operators honed their killing skills under De Kock's watchful eye. They perfected poisons, letter bombs and booby-trapped headphones and cars. And their death toll was countless. In time, De Kock and his team found creative ways of disposing of bodies: a roasting on a fire would suffice if they had time to spare (and perhaps a braai to retire in the meantime); but when they were in a hurry they thought nothing of vapourising their victims with explosives.

An extract from a Sapa report on De Kock's sentencing in 1996 is illuminating:

> A life sentence was also imposed for the 1985 death of Krugersdorp security guard Japie Maponya, "whose only crime was that he had a brother who was an ANC member who was being sought by the police", the judge said.
>
> Maponya was kidnapped, brutally assaulted by several policemen and taken to Swaziland, where he was murdered. De Kock personally bashed in Maponya's head with a spade.
>
> Six years' imprisonment was imposed for defeating the ends of justice in the case where De Kock ordered that explosives be used to destroy the body of Sweet Sambo, who was killed by Komatipoort policemen during questioning at the Squamans police base.

And on and on and on. The damage De Kock and his men wrought was deep and lasting. We should all sleep a little better at night knowing that he is due to spend the rest of his days in C-Max prison in Pretoria. Except that that might not happen.

De Kock claims to have entered negotiations for a presidential pardon in 2009, and there is widespread speculation about his release. The argument goes that he at least attended the TRC, admitted his guilt and acknowledged his wrongdoing, giving some sense of closure to his victims' relatives. Also, he is offering to provide further information about others involved in apartheid-era death squads, including individuals who went "scot-free". If Jacob Zuma is tempted, as many believe he is, to "balance" the potential pardoning of Schabir Shaik with that of De Kock, then it really is on the cards. *(See Schabir Shaik.)*

But it is worth remembering that De Kock's application for amnesty at the TRC was turned down because various murders he committed were not politically motivated. Yes, there remains the very strong suspicion that De Kock's superiors

> "I take full responsibility for all operations carried out by my men while I was commander at Vlakplaas… We have destroyed lives, ruined the lives of the families of those we killed, by living past one another we destroyed one another: it was a futile exercise; we wasted the most precious thing. Life itself."
> *– Eugene de Kock*

> "I wanted to know how he walked into his house after a hit, how did he switch from assassin to father reading bedtime stories to his sons? He said sometimes after an operation he'd drink it out of his mind. Sometimes he'd go home and burn all the clothes he'd been wearing, then wash obsessively…
>
> He talked about the horror that comes back to him at night. How he smells it, tastes it, sees it and he can't sleep. I remember at the time I found that reassuring, such a man shouldn't be able to sleep at night."
> *– Jann Turner, after interviewing De Kock in prison*

were well aware of his activities, or at least chose not to make themselves aware, and he has even gone on record declaring that the chain of command reached all the way to FW de Klerk, who he calls "an unconvicted murderer". But that's hardly the point here. Eugene "Prime Evil" De Kock is in jail, and should remain in that state, because he's a very sick man who was so desensitised to violence that he killed as easily as ordinary people make a ham sandwich.

Dingane

c. 1795 – 1840

King of the Zulus (1828-1840); incompetent military leader; prime instigator of Boer-Zulu antagonism

DINGANE KASENZANGAKHONA ASSUMED THE ZULU THRONE in a typical manner of the day – by murdering the incumbent. He and half-brother Umhlangana waited until King Shaka had sent an impi off to the north to get on with the pillaging and imperialism associated with the Mfecane, then, with security at the king's kraal at a low ebb, the two pounced on their brother and bludgeoned him to death.

Dingane was a king of great proportions, weighing in excess of 150 kilograms, but he certainly wasn't a great king. In fact, after Shaka – who may indeed have been a psychopath but at least had talent *(see Shaka)* – Dingane was dangerously inept, and it was his disastrous dealings with the Voortrekkers and especially one Pieter Retief that ensures his ignominious inclusion here.

Retief was a product of his time; that is to say an arrogant racist who, like all the trekkers, had fled the fairest Cape in order to hang on to his slaves after the meddlesome Brits banned slavery in 1834. He entered KwaZulu in 1837, trundling down the Drakensberg between today's Harrismith and the top of Oliviershoek Pass, with the intention of getting Dingane to grant him and his followers some land so that they might farm.

It was, of course, an astonishing request, and if Dingane had been possessed of an ounce of his brother's intellect he'd have just told Retief to voetsek once and for all, or else. Instead, as though in a moronic 19th-century rendition of *Survivor Zululand*, Dingane chose to set Retief a challenge. Head back over the Drakensberg to retrieve some cattle that had been stolen by the rival Tlokwa people and they were in business, Dingane declared, believing it to be a task Retief could never accomplish. He was wrong.

Retief did what was asked of him and, on his return to Zululand, he rode to Mgungundlovu, Dingane's capital, to sign the deal and celebrate with a two-day feast, having left the older men under his command, along with the women and children, laagered at Weenen and Blaauwkranz. The news of Retief's success had shocked Dingane and by now he had, in his eminent stupidity, concluded that the only solution to the dilemma he'd created was to murder the Boer leader and his men. It was a decision already beset with fateful portent, but it is in the savage detail that Dingane ensured enduring enmity betwixt Boer and Zulu.

Dingane had Retief and his retinue halter their horses and leave their firearms at the entrance to Mgungundlovu, it being against Zulu culture to dance with guns and horses. It is said that, amid the feasting and the dancing, Dingane then leapt to his feet and shouted, *"Babuleli labathakati!"* – Kill the wizards!

"Are you stabbing me, kings of the earth? You will come to an end through killing one another."

– Shaka's last words, allegedly

"You think you will rule this country, but I already see the swallows [whites] coming."

– Also Shaka's last words, allegedly

On Dingane's demand, Retief and his men were dragged out of the kraal, across the Ingwebini stream and out on to the Mahlabathini plain, where they were put to death as wizards. That meant they were impaled by having any number of 12-inch stakes rammed into their rectums. The lucky ones were executed with a knobkerrie to the skull soon afterwards. Some say Retief was last to suffer the sharp suppository, having watched his 13-year-old son be put to death first.

It was gruesome stuff, but Dingane was not done. He then sent an impi to find the laagers at Weenen and Blauwkranz, where they set upon Retief's women and children, murdering them to a soul, including 185 children and 250 slaves.

What had been an ill-considered and presumptuous request for land from Retief, a man who evidently didn't think much of the indigenous population, ended up sinking the deep historical foundation on which so much Afrikaner-Zulu, and even Afrikaner-black, enmity was founded.

The retaliation was devastating. A punitive expedition was organised the following year by fellow trekker Andries Pretorius, which led to the Battle of Blood River on 16 December 1838. Dingane, possessed of none of Shaka's military genius, essentially threw his impis into a deathtrap conjured by the brilliant martial mind of Pretorius, and his army was slaughtered to the point that the Ncome River ran red with the blood of fallen Zulus. Pretorius went on to Mgungundlovu, where he found the corpses of Retief and his entourage along with – rather conveniently – a land treaty that he would allege Dingane had signed with Retief. The Boers now had an "official" claim to the Zulus' land. *(See Andries Pretorius.)*

Meanwhile, Dingane survived Blood River, but at the cost of 3,000 of his troops, including two of the three Zulu princes who had an eye on the Zulu throne. (Three Boers were injured.) The surviving prince, Mpande, another of Shaka's half brothers, teamed up with Pretorius in January 1840 to defeat Dingane's army at the bloody battle of Maqongqe in return for the throne. Dingane, gruesome to the last, was furious with his general Ndlela and had him executed by slow strangulation. He then fled to the east, towards what is now Mozambique. He could run but he couldn't hide; his death came in the Lebombo mountains at the hands of the Swazis and Nyawo, and he was buried under a fig tree. His headstone consists of three rocks.

Dingane was a fat, talentless bully. His brother Shaka may have been a tyrant and a killer, but Shaka – and Mpande – at least had an understanding of the bigger picture. Dingane's unnecessarily brutal treatment of Retief and his followers – and the murder of 185 children at Weenen – was to cast a pall of hatred over South Africa that lingers to this day and still offers white supremacists "evidence" that the Zulu people are inherently savage. It's not the case, obviously. It's just that Dingane was a cruel and arrogant fool of the worst order.

Alec Erwin

b. 17 January 1948

Minister of Trade and Industry (1996-2004) and Public Enterprises (2004-2008); avoider of responsibility; figurehead of the South African energy catastrophe

IN THE MODERN WORLD, ELECTRICITY IS EVERYTHING. It cooks our food, it pumps our water, it runs the computers upon which our work is done. It powers the mines, the factories, the offices and the retail centres. It keeps food cold in the day, it keeps people warm at night and, not least of all, it provides us with the light to avoid tripping over the cat and falling down the stairs. It is in essence the giant iron lung that ventilates the economy. And in the 1990s and early 2000s, our government completely ignored it.

Eskom, under National Party rule, and driven by the paranoid nature of the apartheid state, had always ensured there was a good supply of electricity. This was born out of the laager mentality, the obsession with self-sufficiency. No nearby state would contemplate selling electricity to the white-supremacist regime so Eskom's bosses were tasked with ensuring we always had excess capacity. They built enormous power stations in the Transvaal and Natal and supplied them with coal from the vast coalfields nearby. In fact, they got so into it that they went a bit overboard and several stations had to be mothballed. And then, just to be sure there wouldn't ever be a problem in the Cape if it got cut off from the grid – there's that paranoia again – they got the French to build Africa's only nuclear power station at Koeberg. The Nats had so much cheap electricity at their disposal they didn't know what to do with it, but it helped them sleep at night and it turned out to be one of the rare gems they bequeathed to the new South Africa in 1994. At the time, Eskom was the world's seventh-largest power utility, and it was totally awesome. As fast as the economy could grow, there would easily be enough electricity to power it for a good decade or thereabouts…

Of course, if that growth was to happen, then over the next few years a plan would have to be made for the future. Growth equals more electricity demand which equals more electricity generation required. A fairly simple equation, you'd think.

Now, Thabo Mbeki may have done many things to stuff up the country during his presidency *(see Thabo Mbeki)*, but the one thing he didn't do was ruin the economy. On the contrary, his sane fiscal policies led to rapid growth from the late 1990s right through until the financial crisis of 2008. He can be fairly credited with creating a black middle class, ensuring the happy prosperity of the existing middle class, and improving (in some ways) the lives of millions of South Africans. Using a burgeoning tax revenue his government built houses – millions of them. It electrified vast swathes of South Africa that had previously relied on candles and paraffin. And it cashed in on a great commodities boom, with the mining, processing and construction industries all going great guns. In this way, Mbeki genuinely did preside over a vast improvement in many people's lives, and for this he deserves acknowledgment. But he also presided over the catastrophic decline of our ability to generate electricity efficiently and in sufficient quantities.

"There is not a national energy crisis. There is a tight reserve margin which we are addressing."

– Alec Erwin, 2006

The growing industry sectors and burgeoning middle class, and all those lucky people in their new houses with their new geysers and new lights and new flatscreen TVs, started flicking more switches and turning on more appliances. More and more people were roasting a chicken on any given Sunday or taking a shower on any given Tuesday or running an industrial steel mill 24 hours a day. On top of this, we started exporting electricity to Mozambique and Zimbabwe in an effort to start tapping international markets. Demand soared, a crisis loomed – and Eskom did nothing. Well, that's what a lot of people think anyway.

Actually, Eskom – which was still pretty awesome back then – passed on the news to government that demand was on track to outstrip supply and that it was time to get cracking on some new power stations. They had been banned from building any themselves after a 1998 government proposal to create a competitive private-energy sector came into effect, but the impossible regulations and limitations imposed on potential Independent Power Producers resulted in precisely zero companies putting forth tenders. While the various government ministries and officials ruminated over this little setback in their plans, Eskom's power-station ban remained in place until 2004. Meanwhile, the government directed its funds into unneeded stealth frigates and fourth-generation jet fighters. *(See Joe Modise.)* If this sounds absolutely nuts that's because it is. It's fairies-at-the-bottom-of-thegarden, head-in-the-sand, hey-it's-not-my-problem nuts.

But it was only half the problem. In the meantime, Eskom was becoming increasingly less awesome. The vast pool of skilled personnel that had served the utility was being slowly whittled down by unrealistic affirmative-action requirements; huge amounts of money were being lost due to non-payment of bills by low-income customers and the Zimbabwean government; staff became distracted by the ludicrous Pebble Bed Modular Reactor project, a pie-in-the-sky plan to build and sell small nuclear power stations. Across the country the electrical grid fell into disrepair, and by 2002 Johannesburg alone was suffering around a thousand power cuts a year.

So, who was to blame for the catastrophic run-it-till-it-breaks mentality that had overwhelmed Eskom? Hard to say exactly. Yes, Eskom themselves; simply put they didn't shout loud enough when warning the government of the impending problems. But they certainly did warn them – so to government we look, where Mbeki adds another black mark to his CV. Specifically, though, it took a veritable confederacy of dunces to perform such a sterling demolition job. Take a bow, Ministers of Minerals and Energy Penuell Maduna and Phumzile Mlambo-Ngcuka; wave to the crowds, Ministers of Public Enterprises Stella Sigcau and Jeff Radebe. *(See Stella Sigcau.)*. There were more besides, but if we're going to channel our collective disdain and disbelief into one person, let it be that bumbling fool of an old man Alec Erwin, who came to personify South Africa's electric dysfunctionality in his role as minister of public enterprises between 2004 and 2008. He is by no means responsible for all the ruinous policy that sent Eskom into an inevitable and widely predicted spiral – in fact, some commentators credit him with actually elevating the problem into the spotlight – but he deserves his place here if only for his ineptness and prevarications in dealing with the South African public.

The perilously tight nature of electricity supply in South Africa was illustrated on Christmas Day 2005, when one of the nuclear reactors at Koeberg was suddenly shut down due to damage that would take half a year or more to repair. Koeberg continued to attract trouble over the coming months, and the Western Cape was plunged into chaos as massive rolling blackouts hit the province. Erwin stepped to the fore.

A 15-centimetre bolt had come loose in the turbine, he explained.

"How?" the nation asked.

"This is, in fact, not an accident," he said. "Any interference with an electricity installation is an exceptionally serious crime. It is sabotage."

Sabotage! A direct attack on the state!

Unfortunately for the fantasist Erwin, other facts were coming to light. In reply to a parliamentary question, Minerals and Energy Minister Lindiwe Hendricks explained that eight out of 60 senior professional engineers and seven out of 46 technical managers had resigned from the power station in the previous two years, including people responsible for accident analysis and safety evaluation. She also revealed that eight out of 60 engineering posts were being filled "through the development of junior professional engineers". In other words, Koeberg was being run by a bunch of *laaities* fresh out of university. The National Energy Regulator of South Africa seemed to concur with this conclusion, noting that "general indiscipline" and unacceptable operating practices were rife at the plant and that three of every four power cuts were due to negligence alone.

The sabotage talk had, of course, been a mere ruse to distract the public from the sheer incompetence behind our electricity woes. As 2006 rumbled on, Erwin finally admitted that human error was to blame, but then repeatedly denied that he'd used the word "sabotage".

> "From 2011 to 2016 rolling blackouts are anticipated unless extraordinary steps are taken to accelerate the realisation of the non-Eskom generation and energy-efficiency projects."
> – *Extract from a summary of South Africa's draft integrated resource plan, released by the Department of Energy in October 2010*

His spokeswoman explained the logic: "What the minister said is that if one interferes deliberately with the installation of electricity, it is sabotage. He did not say that the bolt found in the generator in Unit 1 was sabotage."

No-one was fooled. Eskom was falling apart bolt by bolt, and the worst was yet to come.

With the nation rapidly outgrowing its electricity shoe size, 2008 arrived. A scene played out, and it probably went a bit like this: in Umlazi, outside Durban, a much-loved grandmother of six called Gladys Mazibuko turned on her TV to watch an episode of *Generations*, and the switch called Eskom tripped. A perfect storm of ineptitude, lack of foresight and bad luck had come together, and the result was rolling blackouts across the country. Cities plunged into darkness. Factories stopped operating. The mines had to be shut down (because workers wouldn't be able to return to the surface in case of an outage). The economy went bonk.

The government's response, this time, was to blame wasteful consumers. "Go to sleep earlier so that you can grow and be cleverer. Boil less water; use the microwave rather than the stove; take a shower and not a shallow bath," Minerals and Energy Minister Bujelwa Sonjica admonished us.

Under Erwin's watch, Eskom established a team called "demand-side management". This was an international first, a South African invention. For the first time in the history of any money-making organisation, ever, a department within a company was established to find ways to persuade people to purchase less of its product.

Erwin wittered on about the global village, about how electricity was in short supply in other countries too. Damp coal, bad weather, greedy homeowners – everything was to blame for the crisis except the government or Eskom. (Yes, there were coal problems, of Eskom's making.) He spoke of how growth had taken policy-makers by surprise, failing to point out that growth *was* the policy. With his communist's grasp of economics, he wildly denied that the electricity shortage would have an impact on GDP or growth, but as waves of scheduled load shedding washed across the country and things ground to a standstill, billions of rands simply disappeared out of our economy and into the darkness.

In late 2010, Erwin's final embarrassment gasped its dying breaths when the Pebble Bed Modular Reactor programme was officially shut down. Before retiring in 2008, Erwin had been the face of the project, repeatedly (over)stating its viability and prospects, with his flustered comments instilling in any listeners an inevitable sense of foreboding. No-one was surprised to hear the plug was being pulled and that we'd lost R9 billion in the process. Current-affairs programme *Carte Blanche* summed up the general sentiment: "If money wasted on the PBMR project had been ploughed into other projects, South Africa might not be facing its current power shortage and South Africans might be looking forward to less crippling electricity bills."

As it stands, the Eskom crisis is still with us and will be for another seven years or so, according to the experts, even as a R100-billion investment in upgrading our electricity infrastructure (finally) cracks on. While our household electricity costs rocket, the lack of a guaranteed supply and the promise of more rolling blackouts is like a handbrake on the country's economy. The vast damage caused will only be quantifiable in a decade's time when Alec Erwin is, thankfully, a bad memory.

Bartle Frere

29 March 1815 – 29 May 1884

Colonial administrator; High Commissioner for Southern Africa (1877-1880); principal instigator of the Anglo-Zulu War, including British humiliation at Isandlwana; effectively ignited First Anglo-Boer War

SIR HENRY BARTLE EDWARD FRERE, 1st Baronet, was an archetypal Victorian colonial administrator whose belief in the British Empire was as absolute as his disregard for its inhabitants. His breathtaking, almost admirable, arrogance served him well in India but was to have dreadful implications in South Africa.

Frere, like so many well-bred men of his era, was pretty much born into colonial service, and he came of age at the absolute height of British imperialism. Queen Victoria was picking up territories almost by accident as the British Empire spread its tentacles across the world in search of raw materials for the industrial machine that the north of England had become. It was the birth of globalisation, and Victoria owned it.

At the age of 20, Frere went into colonial service in India and, over the following 38 years he was to have a hugely successful career, the epitome of the stolid senior Raj civil servant. In all, he did the good works that colonial administrators liked to do, eternally motivated by Queen and empire. He was knighted in 1857.

After organising an anti-slavery treaty with the Sultan of Zanzibar (say what you like about the Victorians, but they pursued the eradication of slavery with as much endeavour as they did their empire), Frere was despatched to Southern Africa by Lord Carnarvon to be high commissioner and governor of the Cape in 1877, in the way that British governments liked to do. Sir Bartle would have been marked as "a good egg" back home and, what with one bunch of troublesome darkies being the same as the next, the decision to install Frere in Africa as opposed to India would have made perfect sense at Whitehall Palace. Same difference, what what.

This intractable level of thought was a hallmark of Carnarvon's. He saw the solution to the South African question as being the same as that posed in Canada: simply create a confederation, in this case uniting the Cape Colony, Natal and the two Boer republics, the Orange Free State and the Transvaal, under Her Majesty's protective wing. *(See Lord Carnarvon.)*

This was Sir Bartle's task, and Carnarvon expected a man of his talents to have the objective achieved within a year or two. Frere, ever Her Majesty's loyal servant, set about it with an altogether destructive vigour. After despatching the irritant that was the last gasp of the Xhosa nation in the Ninth Xhosa War, he considered the state of Southern Africa and concluded that the biggest threat to Pax Britannica was the Zulus, whose nation bordered the colony of Natal. Hindsight might suggest that Sir Bartle should have rather asked himself a few questions about those Boer republics, which would later express their opinion about Her Majesty's comforting bosom and Frere's mismanagement of their political situation on the slopes of Majuba Hill. But Frere was convinced: the Zulus had to be smashed.

> "Frere interpreted this tide of events [various rebellions of indigenous peoples] as a 'general and simultaneous rising of Kaffirdom against white civilisation' that blocked the way to confederation and needed to be stamped out altogether. Along with his Cape officials, he took the view that as long as independent African chiefdoms were allowed to exist, the danger of a 'black conspiracy' against white authority would be ever present."
> – *Extract from Diamonds, Gold and War by Martin Meredith*

Naturally, and with typical presumption, he underestimated the task at hand. He had no idea that these Zulus were a wholly different enemy to the Xhosa and not, as he wrote, "a bunch of savages armed with sticks". He would soon find out.

Frere had come to the conclusion that Natal could not exist safely and peacefully alongside an openly marshal nation such as the Zulus under King Cetshwayo. For Frere, looking at the situation in South Africa at the time, he figured that Cetshwayo's *amabutho* regiments were running out of enemies on whom they could satisfy their bloodlust. No doubt his mind contemplated the fair folk of genteel Pietermaritzburg, and he felt it best if he rather than Cetshwayo instigated the blood-shedding.

To do so, Frere had to deal with two major problems. The first was persuading his masters in Britain to approve a war on the Zulus, a sticking point that had arisen since the retirement of Lord Carnarvon in early 1878. The new man, Sir Michael Hicks-Beach, wanted to avoid a "native war" at all costs, but Frere of course saw things differently and he cunningly circumvented the concern by making use of the communication delay between the motherland and Cape Town. The telegraph had only been laid as far as the Cape Verde islands by that stage, with messages taking up to three weeks to make it through from there by ship. Frere was thus able to convince his superiors that he needed to respond to events in South Africa without waiting for approval from Britain, whereupon he cleverly timed his movements and even ignored government instructions to bring about the conflict he desired.

Getting Cetshwayo to fight was another matter altogether, as Zulu and Brit had lived in relative peace and harmony alongside each other in KwaZulu and Natal for years. There was even regular trade between the two, and the British could move through Zululand without harassment. Cetshwayo may have been unpleasant enough to re-impose some of Shaka's more brutal traditions upon his people, such as the Washing of the Spears, by which a Zulu man could effectively not marry until he had bathed his assegai in the blood of an enemy, but he wasn't stupid enough to pick a fight with Victoria, the Great White Queen.

> "His [Frere's] 'ultimatum' was I think the most arrogant piece of despotic rule I have seen in my time."
> – *Anthony Trollope, Victorian novelist who travelled to South Africa in 1877, in letter to a friend dated September 1879*

So Frere, having failed in an attempt to initiate war earlier in the year, gave Cetshwayo an ultimatum, delivered in December 1878, to the king's dumbfounded indunas at a little place on the Thukela (Tugela) River known to this day as the Ultimatum Tree. The tree itself died twenty-odd years ago, but the contents of the ultimatum went down in history.

Frere demanded, in the name of a queen who had never heard of the Zulus and didn't know where Zululand was, and in the name of a government that had specifically instructed him to avoid war, that Cetshwayo disband his *amabutho*, that he stop the practice of the Washing of the Spears, that he allow British colonial involvement in Zululand and, finally, that he pay compensation for what Frere referred to as constant border infractions. It was designed to be impossible. Cetshwayo sent a message to Frere, in the words of historian David Rattray, "begging his British friends not to go to war, and warning him that if the Great White Queen sent her red soldiers into Zululand, his *amabutho* would eat those red soldiers up. The die was cast."

Under Lord Chelmsford, the British invaded Zululand on New Year's Day 1879. By the afternoon of 22 January, nearly 1,400 British and colonial troops and as many as 6,000 Zulu warriors lay dead at the foot of a sphinx-shaped mountain called iSandlwana (subsequently anglicised to the Isandlwana we know today). The eerie twilight of an eclipse of the sun cast a spooky pall over the massacre; with only 55 white soldiers escaping, it was the greatest ever defeat in British colonial history. But it was a pyrrhic victory for Cetshwayo, as the cream of his army – the *indluyengwe* ("the leopard's lair") and the *ingobamakhosi* ("the benders of the kings") – was left dead and dying on the battlefield.

By humiliating Chelmsford (who didn't participate in the battle), Frere and the British Empire, Cetshwayo had "pulled the tail of the greatest lion that ever walked the earth", as Rattray would describe it. Retribution was swift and violent. In July of 1879 Cetshwayo's impi was destroyed at Ulundi. This time the British came prepared, with Gatling guns, cavalry and lancers. It was slaughter.

For Frere, however, it was too late. The stories of Isandlwana – stories of mutilation and disembowelment – shocked and appalled Victorian high society. "What," demanded William Gladstone from the opposition benches, "was the crime of the Zulu?" Frere fruitlessly defended himself against accusations that he'd acted recklessly and without authority. To his great shame, he was censured by Whitehall and then replaced by Sir Garnet Wolseley before the war was out.

Meanwhile, the Boers had come to resent Frere's governing policies, leading to the First Anglo-Boer War in 1880-1881, further humiliating defeats for the British and the effective independence of the Transvaal. Frere's opprobrium was complete.

As for Zululand, it was divided into 17 small compartments, its army disbanded and its people brought under the crown. Cetshwayo was exiled to London, where he had an audience with Victoria, while his kingdom descended into blood feuds and civil war. Cetshwayo returned in 1883 to a ruined nation. He died in February 1884, some say of sadness.

Frere died three months later, in Wimbledon, of a "severe chill", having spent the last years of his life defending his actions in Africa. His arrogance and disregard for the lives of ordinary people had destroyed Zululand and pitched two nations into a war neither had wanted. He bore the cross of Isandlwana until his death.

The guy I sat next to at the polo

Narrow-minded white South African who genuinely believes "they" were better off under apartheid rule

SOMETIMES PEOPLE JUST NEED TO get out more, to take a step out of their closeted space and their familiar surrounds. This can often be an entirely mental process that does not even require you to leave your seat. It doesn't require great intellect even, or a vast repository of knowledge. Really, all it needs is a *soupçon* of empathy.

But this is the thing with racists. Racism most often does not manifest itself with acts of violence or hurtful language. It appears, more cruelly sometimes, as indifference; that deep-seated inability to care. And if you just don't care, what's the point of setting foot outside your carefully constructed intellectual laager? What's the point of trying out another point of view for size? I mean, why would you?

The guy I sat next to at the polo a couple of years back was just such a man. Argentina was in the process of dismantling South Africa a great many goals to nil but, as is often the case at these high-society sporting events, it's really not done to care about the polo at Inanda – which is how my wife and I found ourselves eating posh food at a table with some very rich young people wearing clothes worth more than the average South African's car. The Springboks had recently won the World Cup under the leadership of John Smit and Jake White, and the latter had resigned. This is what filled our conversation.

White had famously butted heads with the politically appointed bosses of South African rugby and knew that once the cup was delivered to South Africa his days were numbered. This, of course, was ridiculous. To reward a coach for winning a World Cup with an old-fashioned sacking is plain madness, but this is the way with sports administrators in South Africa. They wish to mould the game for their own benefit and to suit their political and racial agendas. White was not malleable and he was, of course, white. He had to go.

The issue of the transformation of sports in South Africa is made doubly irritating by the polarisation of opinion – those who would force "quota players" through because of their race, and those who punt the racial status quo under the shabby veil of merit. The guy who sat next to me at the polo was just such a guy.

"No, man," he said loudly, ignoring the melanin-rich nature of one of the female guests at the table. "Rugby is a game played by whites. It should be run by whites. Blacks don't care about rugby. You don't see me complaining that there aren't enough whites playing for Bafana Bafana."

Now, I perhaps could have fathomed a comment like this from an old white *bittereinder* who'd lived the majority of his years under the crippling indoctrination of apartheid rule, but this was a young man, in his early thirties, who had evidently never bothered to think outside of the northern suburbs of Johannesburg. He was born into a profoundly changing political landscape; he would have been in his teens when Mandela went free. And yet it never occurred to him that his thought processes were couched in the dogma of a bygone era (or even that he should refrain from expressing them in the company of others). The more polo guy talked, the more he became a caricature of detachment from the reality that is South Africa outside of those precious, closeted few square kilometres between Johannesburg and Sandton.

> "Soccer in South Africa is a black sport, Rugby is a white sport, full stop... Klaar gepraat."
>
> – *Leon, online post*

When controversial *Sunday Times* columnist Bareng-Batho Kortjaas wrote that he felt no joy in the Springbok victory in 2007, it attracted furious responses from many people. Had he read it, polo guy would have been just one of those people. But, while Kortjaas's sentiment is hugely disappointing, surely it is understandable? After all, there wasn't one black man on the field. (Bryan Habana and JP Pietersen were the only two "previously disadvantaged" players in the match squad.) The critical problem here is that polo guy, with his limited thought processes and his inability to empathise, creates opinions like Kortjaas's. He is the source of them.

Polo guy can't have it both ways. We either do all this stuff together, really try to participate in sport (and life) together, in which case Kortjaas and his ilk will one day feel included in the great spectacle that is Springbok rugby, or we stick to his dream of racial segregation in sport and stay rooted in the past, with all the misery that brings.

Polo guy was very well dressed, smartly groomed and rather good-looking. His key fob bore the Mercedes-Benz logo. His strikingly pretty blonde wife didn't look like she had too much between her ears, but nonetheless she was strikingly pretty and blonde – and she agreed vehemently with everything he had to say. Which is to say that this man has been played a great hand in life. He's in the perfect position to make a real difference in this country – and yet he's exactly the person we don't need here; the type of person holding us back; the type of person who justifies the similarly delusional thinking of our post-World Cup rugby administrators.

Unfortunately there are countless polo guys out there, still clinging on desperately to the past, still trying to stop the black masses from breaching their laager. After all, it's just so nice without them there, isn't it?

Steve Hofmeyr

b. 29 August 1964
Afrikaans singer and soap star; self-appointed voice of
the Afrikaans nation; high-profile racist

STEVE HOFMEYR'S MUSIC MAY BE DREADFUL, but look, that's not good enough for entry into this book. There are loads of hugely successful Afrikaans music artists who churn out derivative, formulaic junk on a daily basis. The poppies love it, and that's really okay. So he's here for the soapies, then? Or is it the philandering? Or the "assault" on the magazine editor?

None of that. (His acting wasn't bad, actually.)

Steve's here because he has, in his later years, become an ugly South African stereotype with – as he characterises it – a pale skin. He's here because of his deeply ingrained racism. Because he's so stupid that he allowed a deeply limited punk like Julius Malema to wheedle it out of him.

When Malema was at the height of his pre-World Cup exhortations that people go out and kill farmers and all the rest, Hofmeyr's reaction was, from a PR point of view, perfectly, immaculately wrong. Hofmeyr has, for some reason, decided to install himself as spokesman for oppressed under-siege Afrikanerdom. When white people are murdered he feels the burning hot rage of Blaauwkranz and Weenen. Not so much, it appears, when black people are murdered.

But how do we know it's about race? Well, Hofmeyr was stupid enough to pen a letter to Malema, in which he opined that, in fact, Malema really wants to be white, and disguises it with hateful utterances. In March 2010, he wrote:

> Yours is mere envy disguised as hatred as nothing you say, wear, drive and steal, even your idiocy, is a luxury born of this continent. You must appeal to base sentiment as Africa has yet to yield a single intellectual, a single thought school, a single intellectual thought not inspired by the very West you and Mugabe detest.

He went on:

To be proud you must pander to white ideas: you must drive cars, live in expensive hotels, wear suits, be Christian, do unions, be Communist, wear wigs, speak English and play soccer.

It's shocking stuff. To respond to Malema's utterly base gibberings with utterly base gibberings of his own were not the actions of an intelligent man. They were the actions of a man who has allowed a pipsqueak to expose him for what he is – somebody whose real motivations are evident in his hypocrisy. Truth is, the acting may be fine and the music may be bad – but the politics, Steve, really, are just terrible.

"Steve, in his infinite wisdom, decided he would be the mouthpiece of all white South Africans and write Malema a racist-fuelled letter. Just so you know Steve, I would sooner let my sh*t-devouring dogs speak on my behalf before I allowed you to do so."

– Ayo, online post

And here's the problem: Steve Hofmeyr has fans. Lots of them. People who – a frightening thought – actually listen to what he has to say. These are the people who think that the horrors of apartheid should have been forgotten on 27 April 1994. It's been 16 years already, they say. And yet the same people remember the antics of Kitchener and Milner 110 years ago with true and righteous fury. (Afrikaners, Hofmeyr wrote in the same letter to Malema, are "the only tribe to sacrifice a third of its population to breathe in the African air".)

It's scary, low-brow, unsophisticated, victimhood-laced stuff, and there's too much of it in South Africa. As one commentator at the time remarked: it's a case of dumb and dumber. Which is Malema and which is Hofmeyr – like Orwell's pigs and men – is impossible to say.

Genuinely traumatic as it is to contemplate, Steve Hofmeyr is better off left to the singing.

(See Julius Malema.)

Sol Kerzner

b. 23 August 1935

Hotel and gambling magnate; founder of Sun City;
slick operator; apartheid profiteer

SOL KERZNER'S A REMARKABLE MAN. It's just a pity he had to head off and be remarkable elsewhere. Not surprising, though.

Born in the poor Johannesburg suburb of Troyeville into a poor family of Jewish-Ukrainian immigrants, Solomon Kerzner would eventually become staggeringly rich. It started with an audacious five-star hotel in Umhlanga Rocks when Umhlanga was nothing but a couple of shacks by the sea, and soon became Southern Sun International, a franchise of hotels that would eventually revolutionise the southern African hospitality industry.

But it was 1979 that really changed things for our Sol. He negotiated a deal with Bophuthatswana's tinpot president Lucas Mangope – a deal that smelt particularly fishy – which granted him an exclusive gambling licence in the "independent" Bantustan and the rights to build an enormous casino. Sol had a dream: to bring a slice of Las Vegas to South Africa and to make a mint. It was outrageous and it was brilliant, and it worked.

Though it was a huge risk at the time, Sol's logic was, in retrospect, very sound – if deeply cynical. Topless revue shows and gambling were anathema to the Calvinist apartheid government of the time and, of course, banned in South Africa, but with Bophuthatswana being nominally independent, the good people of Johannesburg and Pretoria were now just an hour or so away from a temple of sin – and they came flooding in. The massive musical acts and boxing matches that Sol managed to draw in from abroad provided a further lure; playing in South Africa was inexcusable but Bop was deemed acceptable by many performers, especially if the money was right.

Kerzner went massively, hugely kitsch at Sun City, and he attained even more stratospheric heights of camp in 1992 when he completed the Palace of the Lost City, replete with artificial rainforests and waterfalls, a beach, a sea with real waves, "The Bridge of Time" and a world-class Gary Player-designed golf course, famously equipped with real crocodiles.

Sun City really is quite ridiculous. It's so extremely over the top that South Africans have come to love it for its fantastic otherworldliness and the sheer chutzpah required to build a kitsch Hollywood "lost city" in the middle of the bush in North West province, far from anywhere that really matters.

But Sol – the foul-mouthed, hard-drinking, skirt-chasing hospitality magnate renowned for starting meetings with the line, "What the fuck is going on here?" – is one of those personalities whose very being seems to ooze scheme and scandal. He was accused by many of propping up Bantustan dictators and profiting from apartheid policies. The song *(I Ain't Gonna Play) Sun City* was eventually released to protest his very creation, becoming an anti-apartheid anthem.

"For white South Africans, Bop had for years been their vacation from the Calvinist restraints of their own society. In the homeland's luxuriously kitschy Sun City resort, they came to gamble, carouse with black prostitutes and watch pornographic movies. Vast sums of cash brought in the Miss World pageant, international golf, world-title boxing fights and musicians, all of whom, with a nod and wink, finessed the sports and cultural boycott of pariah South Africa by visiting 'independent' Bophuthatswana."
– *From The Bang-Bang Club by Greg Marinovich and Joao Silva*

Sol's later career abroad was described as follows by *The Evening Standard*: "Each time he has sought to open a casino in a new territory, his controversial reputation has travelled before him and he has had to convince the local gaming board he is a person to be trusted. Each time he has eventually prevailed."

Exactly how Sol has prevailed is not speculated in the article, but anyone who knows his history in South Africa won't mind hazarding a guess. Besides the Mangope shenanigans, the other major scandal back in the day related to a bribe of R2 million paid to George Matanzima, prime minister of the Transkei, for exclusive gambling rights in his homeland, which he then dished out among his ministers. *(See Stella Sigcau.)* Matanzima was later forced out of office and then jailed for his role, while efforts to extradite Sol to face the music proved futile. Allegations were later put forward by Bantu Holomisa, among others, that Sol had attempted to have his name cleared with a R2-million donation to the ANC, along with regular displays of largesse to senior party members. Not much came of it in the end, but Sol took the hint, sold Sun City and skedaddled off overseas just in time to miss democracy.

He went on to build an enormous, and enormously impressive, new empire.

Based in the Bahamas, it is even more improbable and absurd than what he left behind in South Africa. His pride and joy is a R15-billion casino-hotel, the Atlantis on Paradise Island, which is set amid the world's biggest man-made aquarium.

Impressive indeed, but having made a mint out of the circumstances created by apartheid, old Sol – the Sun King, South Africa's Donald Trump, the Bugsy Siegel of the Veld – could perhaps have stayed invested in South Africa instead of taking his vast amounts of money abroad. Admittedly, though, the old man has now dipped a toe back in our waters with his not-quite-revolting One & Only resort in Cape Town – are we happy to have him back?

Lord Kitchener

24 June 1850 – 5 June 1916

British Field Marshal; commander of imperial forces during the Second Anglo-Boer War (1900-1902); pioneer of scorched-earth policy and concentration camps; fomenter of English-Afrikaans animosity

THE SECOND ANGLO-BOER WAR – once the Boer War, now often referred to as the South African War – was a particularly nasty affair that, to this day, has a powerful ability to stir up emotions. The British and Germans, for example, largely get on very well 65 years after the Second World War despite the litany of Nazi atrocities or the much-maligned carpet-bombing of German civilians that took place. And yet for some Afrikaners "the English", by which they mean the British, are just about the worst people on God's planet. They're a nation of thieves that hounded the Afrikaans people across the interior of their God-given place in Africa, offering 150 years of harassment that eventually drove these peace-loving pioneers, in desperation, to bear arms on the slopes of Talana Hill, at Ladysmith and on Spioenkop.

Much of that lingering enmity, more than a century later, can be laid squarely at the feet of he with that most impressive of moustaches, Field Marshal Horatio Herbert Kitchener, 1st Earl Kitchener, KG, KP, GCB, OM, GCSI, GCMG, GCIE, ADC, PC*.

Kitchener – who would later gain universal recognition as the iconic pointing general on First World War recruitment posters – came to South Africa in 1899 along with the huge number of reinforcements sent from Britain to quell the Boer uprising. By late 1900 the Boers had lost the conventional war, despite inflicting serious casualties upon the British. General Roberts moved on, and Kitchener became commander-in-chief.

Kitchener negotiated a reconciliatory settlement with Boer leaders, but this was

---

* Respectively: Order of the Garter, Order of St Patrick, Grand Cross of the Bath, Order of Merit, Order of the Star of India, Order of St Michael and St George, Order of the Indian Empire, Aide-de-Camp, Privy Council of the United Kingdom.

shot down by the British cabinet, so he chose to extend and refine a systematic scorched-earth policy to counter the guerrilla tactics that the Boers were employing. As far as Kitchener was concerned – and he was right – the commandos were getting their sustenance from their farms and families, so British troops laid waste to everything in their path, killing livestock, burning crops, razing farmsteads, poisoning wells and salting fields. They also rounded up whomever they found – men, women and children – and locked them up in internment camps where they could be prevented from aiding the enemy.

Militarily, of course, the strategy was a success. But in the camps it went horribly, appallingly wrong. The British Army was simply not prepared to take care of thousands of civilian prisoners of war. Supplies were thin and before long detainees started to die. Inadequate shelter, poor hygiene, meagre rations and overcrowding allowed malnutrition and diseases such as measles, pneumonia and dysentery to

> "Every one of these children who died as a result of the halving of their rations, thereby exerting pressure onto their family still on the battle-field, was purposefully murdered. The system of half rations stands exposed and stark and unshamefully as a cold-blooded deed of state policy employed with the purpose of ensuring the surrender of people whom we were not able to defeat on the battlefield."
>
> – *WT Stead, British journalist and fierce critic of the Boer War. (A close friend of Cecil John Rhodes, he went down with the Titanic in 1912.)*

sweep through the camps, eventually killing an estimated 28,000 inmates. The final figure may not be as affecting in the light of the 20th-century slaughter that was to follow across so much of the world, but in context it was devastating: it equated to roughly a quarter of all interred Afrikaners and included more than half the Boer child population. A further 20,000 or more black war refugees died under similar conditions in segregated camps, a shamefully overlooked tragedy. By comparison, the Boers lost about 7,000 combatants and the British 22,000.

Kitchener was accused at the time of attempting genocide – of intentionally creating the conditions so that Boer children would die – but the likely truth is that he, in his typical manner, was just focused on winning the war. He was tasked with defeating an astute and stubborn enemy and he didn't consider conditions in the camps to be a high priority. It wasn't genocide, but it is one of the two most horrifying cases of murderous negligence and indifference in South Africa's history. *(See Thabo Mbeki and Manto Tshabalala-Msimang.)*

In Britain many people were horrified, and the government came in for severe criticism, especially after reports made by Emily Hobhouse, the Englishwoman who exposed conditions in the camps, became public. The wheels turned slowly at Westminster, but eventually the arch-conservative British high commissioner Alfred Milner was ordered to take the camps into civilian hands and reduce the mortality rate, which he did with relative ease. By then it was, tragically, far too late – and it ultimately proved how unnecessary the loss of life had been.

Kitchener, a smart (if remarkably callous) operator, used the uproar concerning the camps to his advantage. He made a great show of bowing to liberal demands in Britain that he stop interring Boer families; instead, while continuing his destructive scorched-earth policy, he simply left them on their ruined farms, thus abrogating the responsibility of their survival to the commandos. In a stroke, Kitchener had made the care of displaced woman and children the Boers' problem. It was a brilliant way to put pressure onto General Louis Botha and company, but it was also desperately cruel as, by then, life in the camps was no longer a death sentence, whereas life in the veld was exceptionally harsh.

> "When children are being treated in this way and dying, we are simply ranging the deepest passions of the human heart against British rule in Africa. It will always be remembered that this is the way British rule started there, and this is the method by which it was brought about."
> – *David Lloyd George, future prime minister of the UK, responding to reports of internment camp conditions in South Africa, in June 1901*

In the end Kitchener's calculating ruthlessness worked; Boer commandos and their families found it harder and harder to survive, and the war came to a close with the signing of the Treaty of Vereeniging on 31 May 1902. To his credit, Kitchener outmanoeuvred Milner during the negotiation process, overriding the high commissioner's contemptible intentions to forcibly anglicise Afrikaners, and arranging limited self-government and a reconstruction grant for the former Boer republics. The Transvaal and the Orange Free State were now British, and the Union of South Africa followed in 1910.

Kitchener's brutal application of the scorched-earth policy would have a lasting impact, forcing many Afrikaners off their ruined farms and into the burgeoning metropolis of Johannesburg, where they joined the ranks of destitute and unskilled labourers. Afrikaner-English relations had been disastrously damaged, laying the foundations for the rise of Afrikaner nationalism over the next half-century.

For any nation to lose half its children in a matter of months would be a holocaust. It is hard to imagine such grief, and it is that, more than anything, that today still raises fury and sorrow in Afrikaner hearts. Though a more objective judge might place Milner at the top of the pile, it is no surprise that Kitchener takes his position as the most hated man in Afrikanerdom, the archetypal *rooinek* who wrought misery on the volk. His complete indifference to the plight of those in the camps and his ruthless focus on winning at any cost was, in the final analysis, unconscionable, cruel and wholly unnecessary.

(See Lord Milner.)

Louis Luyt

b. 18 June 1932

Businessman and rugby administrator; president of the
South African Rugby Football Union (1994-1998); face
of the ugly South African

THERE'S A PARTICULARLY CUTTING SKETCH you can watch on YouTube by the British comedy puppet show *Spitting Image*. It's called "I've never met a nice South African", and it's an enlightening product of its time – 1986 – when the apartheid Saffer was the pariah of the world. Released just after PW Botha had failed to cross the Rubicon and was implementing his state of emergency instead, the song is characteristically savage. It talks of South Africans – meaning white South Africans – as a "bunch of talentless murderers who smell like baboons", "arrogant bastards who hate black people" and "ignorant loudmouths with no sense of humour". (It is, a quarter century later, really quite funny.)

Such thoughts, no doubt, went through the minds of the New Zealand rugby team and delegation at the dinner to celebrate the end of the 1995 Rugby World Cup. Let there be no doubt of the event's significance. It was a glorious moment in this country, and now Morgan Freeman has even done a movie emphasising just that. That's why it takes an individual of rare mean spirit to leave a bitter taste in the mouth after such a special day. Louis Luyt was his name, and he turned out to be the turd in the punchbowl. Because here was a guy who didn't know how to win with any grace.

Speaking at the gala dinner, Luyt, president of the South African Rugby Football Union (Sarfu) at the time, opined that not only was it good and right that the Springboks had won the cup, but had they been allowed to play, they would have won the last two as well – one of which, of course, the All Blacks had won. Luyt was doing the spitting image of the *Spitting Image* South African who no-one can abide. He was being a deeply unfunny, egotistical loudmouth. Famously, the Kiwis walked out of the dinner and went back to their hotel.

Louis Luyt had made his fortune as a fertiliser salesman in the 1960s. Some say he was so good at his job that there are still farmers in the Karoo with stockpiles of his stuff. Unfortunately, however, he didn't stick to his calling. Presumably, he had some charms back then and the money went to his head, turning him into the boorish megalomaniac South Africans would come to know once he'd wangled his way in to the presidency of Sarfu. He spent five years in the role, a period in which he conducted himself as the untouchable king of rugby, dismissive of any and all outsider opinion or sensitivity. It was, and still is, remarkable that such an unpleasant and divisive man could hold this important position for so long, and it was no surprise when it all ended in scandal and brouhaha and his forced resignation in 1998.

A pollster is taking opinions outside the Union Buildings in Pretoria. He approaches four men waiting to cross the road. One is a Saudi, one is a Russian, one is a North Korean, and the other is Louis Luyt.

"Excuse me," says the pollster, "I would like your opinion on the current meat shortage."

The Saudi replies, "Excuse me, but what is a shortage?"

The Russian replies, "Excuse me, but what is meat?"

The North Korean replies, "Excuse me, but what is an opinion?"

And Louis Luyt says, "Excuse me, but what is 'Excuse me'?"

– *From Leon Schuster's Lekker, Thick South African Joke Book*

Along the way, he unconscionably dragged Nelson Mandela into court to testify in a commission of enquiry into rugby in 1996. It was a humiliating moment for many South Africans, the first time the man who freed the country had been in a witness box since the Rivonia Trial of 1964, and it came only a few years after Luyt was justifiably accused of racism when, during the Springboks' first match after readmission, against New Zealand at Ellis Park in 1992, the Tannoy played *Die Stem* in a "deliberate breach of a pledge not to promote apartheid symbols". These boorish acts were, it seems, perfectly in character for the man because Luyt, back in the 1970s, had been central to an assault on South African media by the apartheid government.

At the time, the state was becoming increasingly fed up with so-called liberal newspapers, such as the *Rand Daily Mail*. In response, Minister of Information Connie Mulder and State President BJ Vorster attempted to buy SAAN, the holding company behind the *Mail* and the *Sunday Times*. Luyt was their front man. When that failed, Mulder secretly, and again illegally, gave millions of rands to Luyt in order that he set up a pro-government newspaper. He went ahead. It was called the *Citizen*, and it's still going today. Unsurprisingly, the paper's editorial direction was decidedly pro-National Party, the only English-language paper with that particular sentiment.

In time the secret got out, reported – in a rather delicious irony – by the *Rand Daily Mail*. It was known as the Information Scandal, and it probably cost Mulder the presidency. Vorster himself was eventually forced to quit, too. *(See BJ Vorster.)*

Once he had been finally, mercifully ejected from the corridors of power at Sarfu headquarters, Luyt went on to pursue the ultimate vanity project: he started his own political party. The Federal Alliance, established to protect "the rights and integrity of Afrikaners", contested its first election in 1999 – but no-one was particularly surprised when it folded shortly thereafter, having won no seats. After all, who would want to support a front man for apartheid state propaganda, a decidedly offensive after-dinner speaker and a man with questionable views on his melanin-rich compatriots? Luyt the Lout really is, much to our impoverishment, straight out of *Spitting Image*.

DF Malan

22 May 1874 – 7 February 1959

*Prime Minister of South Africa (1948-1954); Dutch
Reformed minister; Nazi sympathiser; champion of
Afrikaner nationalism; apartheid pioneer*

HISTORY IS FULL OF PEOPLE who were somehow able to rationalise their religiosity
with their decidedly ungodly politics and actions. Indeed, they count among
their number some truly wicked people who have performed some of the more
egregious deeds in history.

In the South African context, one can only wonder whether Daniel Francois
Malan, an ordained minister, really was asking himself what Jesus would have
done when he assumed the reins of our country's government in 1948, or whether
his mind had become so overwhelmed by the unpleasant cocktail of opinions that
spawned Afrikaner nationalism that he had completely lost sight of Him. After all,
this was a man who counted among his convictions pro-Nazi leanings, strident
anti-British sentiments, enduring Boer War bitterness and various ropey, made-
for-purpose mythologies about the God-given right of the Afrikaner to rule the
land.

Of all the apartheid leaders, Malan had the fewest excuses. He was a highly
educated man, with degrees in maths and science. Apparently filled with Christian
conviction, Malan joined a seminary and studied to be a minister. He also gained
an MA in philosophy and a doctorate in divinity at Utrecht in the Netherlands. You
might expect, therefore, that Malan would have developed into a worldly, open-
minded Christian. Sadly, that was not the case, and he turned out to be a man of
his era. He was born three years before the first annexation of the Transvaal, and
he was 26 at the outbreak of the Second Anglo-Boer War, the duration of which he
spent in the pro-Boer Netherlands.

On his return to South Africa in 1905, Malan was ordained as a minister in the
Dutch Reformed Church and served in this capacity at various locations across
the country over the next ten years. While performing his missionary work,
Malan became increasingly concerned by the plight of poor white Afrikaners. He
also began quietly agitating for the status of Afrikaans to be elevated to an official

language, as opposed to Dutch. (This was achieved in 1925.) His move into politics came in 1915 when he was asked to edit Cape Town's new daily newspaper, *Die Burger*, the mouthpiece of Barry Hertzog's fledgling National Party. Fast-forward another two decades to a time that saw Malan riding a steady wave of Afrikaner nationalism, and the critical moment in his career came with the fusion of Hertzog's National Party and Jan Smuts's South African Party in 1934 into the United Party. It was a surprising and unwieldy political compromise that was resented bitterly by Malan and his ilk. The result was the relaunching of the National Party as the party that South Africans know today, with Malan as its head. He spent the next 14 years in opposition, but it was only a few years later that Malan was to express so alarmingly clearly what this new, purified National Party stood for.

"[It] is only on the basis of apartheid in regard to residential areas that we shall be able to achieve sound relationships between the one race and the other. Only on that basis will we be able to secure justice for both sides. What justice is there for the non-European if he is in the position in which he is today? He will always have a sense of inferiority. He is unable to do justice to himself. On the basis of apartheid, however, with his own residential area, he will be in a position to do justice to himself. There he will be able to live his own life – there he can develop what is his own, and only by the maintenance and the development of what is your own can you uplift yourself and uplift your people."

– *DF Malan, 1950*

In 1938, the Great Trek was commemorated with a re-enactment that saw nine ox wagons departing from Cape Town and trekking upcountry, an event that was enthusiastically celebrated by Afrikaners across the country. The wagon routes diverged, with one party heading towards Pretoria, where the impressive Voortrekker monument was under construction, and another heading to the site of the Battle of Blood River, where Malan made a landmark speech on the hundred-year anniversary of Andries Pretorius's victory over Dingane's troops. It crystalised the philosophy behind his Afrikaner nationalism.

"At the Blood River battlefield you stand on sacred soil," he declared to the crowd. "It is here that the future of South Africa as a civilised Christian country and the continued existence of the responsible authority of the white race was decided… You stand today in your own white laager at your own Blood River, seeing the dark masses gathering around your isolated white race."

Malan is thought to have been referring to urbanised Afrikaners, who faced competition from black workers. He went on to insist that if there was "no salvation, the downfall of South Africa as a white man's country" would be confirmed. And he, DF Malan, wasn't about to let that happen to the volk, whom he believed God had chosen to prosper in this land.

The battle of Blood River thus re-mythologised *(see Dingane and Andries Pretorius)*, fate was to throw Malan's party just the crowbar he required to prise power from Smuts. It came in the guise of South Africa's entry into the Second World War, which came after much political debate and which ultimately served to emphasise the resentment that Afrikaners felt at being tied to Britain's coat-tails. Such sentiment among Afrikaans voters would eventually propel Malan and the editor of that powerfully anti-British publication *Die Transvaler*, a fellow named Verwoerd, into government three years after the war ended.

The "salvation" Malan had referred to in his speech ten years earlier implied a committed intervention to South Africa's political and socioeconomic status quo. That intervention was to come in the form of apartheid. In 1943, Malan's old ally, *Die Burger*, had first used the word, and the man himself became the first person to mention the term in parliament the following year. So he had promised apartness, and now, in 1948, South Africans would get it.

Malan was 74 when he came to power, but age had neither mellowed him nor ameliorated his convictions. It hadn't blunted the strength of his desire to mould South Africa into the halcyon, sepia-tinged paradise promised by God on the 16th of December 1838. On the contrary, his advanced age served to conjoin the actions of that day, which his older relatives would have recalled with clarity, to the time in which he ruled 110 years later – with, it need hardly be said, tragic consequences.

Malan would leave much of the mechanics of his government to younger men in his administration *(see Hendrik Verwoerd)*, but it was this man, who was really from a different era, who presided paternalistically over those first years of apartheid and the beginning of the apocalyptic legislative assault on black South Africans. Is it any surprise that the first major street renamed in Johannesburg was DF Malan Drive? Not really.

Malan, born in 1874, still haunts us.

Julius Malema

b. 1983

President of the ANC Youth League; pin-up boy for
black racism, tenderpreneurship and the implosion of
rational political debate in South Africa

JULIUS MALEMA'S A FAT LITTLE MAN. How he got so fat is obvious. He is fat because he's got lots of government-tender money and no class whatsoever, and the classless rich always get fat. In Malemaville, Limpopo, KFC is gourmet and obesity, in the absence of an enlightened mind, is said to speak of significance.

Of course, it doesn't help to resort to personal insults. It's best to debate the facts but, as the KFC Kid knows so well, it sure makes you feel better. After all, when Kiddi Amin was engaging in the first real salvos in his war against Jacob Zuma by espousing the genius of Zanu-PF's ruinous land-reform programme in Zimbabwe, he reacted with much vitriol when challenged by a BBC journalist.

Malema had described Zimbabwe's opposition MDC as "Mickey Mouse", and had mocked their "air-conditioned offices in Sandton", to which the BBC's Jonah Fisher pointed out that Malema himself lived in Sandton. Well, it struck a nerve, and instead of being smart about it and responding that there's nothing wrong with a successful South African citizen residing in Sandton, as opposed to a foreign political party, he went ballistic.

The problem with going ballistic is that it shows all your cards. It's your best work. This, in your fury, when you really, really care, is everything you've got. Forget *in vino veritas*. When a man's truly angry, you're going to see to the centre of his soul. Which, in this particular case, was illustrative for the rest of us.

Malema accused the journalist of having a small penis, saying whatever was under his "trouser" was "rubbish". This was intellectual shock and awe, Malema-style. A slam-dunk tour-de-force of off-the-cuff critical political thought from the man who would be president.

In this little moment, young Julius had exposed his hatred of media and their questions, his utter disregard for how he makes South Africa look from abroad and, of course, the scale of the rancour and poison at the heart of how he thinks. He had made it clear that what he lacks in intellect he makes up for in a vicious hate-filled demagoguery, choosing victims of least resistance, the obvious targets – because young Julius is the playground bully who learnt nothing at school other than how to steal the other kids' Milo. So it's the media. It's the mines and their owners. It's white people in general and farmers specifically.

The ANC's struggle history has gifted the likes of Malema a song that contains the exhortation to "shoot the boer, kill the farmer", giving him a deeply shabby, quasi-cultural excuse to encourage people to hate (at best) and murder (at worst) others because of the colour of their skin. It is, of course, vindictive and dangerous, and were it born out of a long and deep personal struggle to free South Africa's poor from apartheid, it would at least give some context to Malema's seemingly bottomless font of racial bile. But it isn't.

> **Malema:** This is a building of a revolutionary party, and you know nothing about the revolution. So here you behave or else you jump!
> **Fisher:** [laughter]
> **Malema:** Don't laugh! Chief, can you get security to remove this thing here? If you're not going to behave, you're [sic] going to call security to take you out. This is not a newsroom this, this is a revolutionary house, and you don't come here with that tendency. Don't come here with that white tendency. Not here. You can do it somewhere else. Not here. If you've got a tendency of undermining blacks even where you work, you are in the wrong place. Here you are in the wrong place. And you can go out. You can go out.
> **Fisher:** [interjecting] That's rubbish. That's absolute rubbish.
> **Malema:** Rubbish is what you have covered in that trouser. That is rubbish. That which you have covered in this trouser is rubbish. Okay? You are a small boy, you can't do anything.
> **Fisher:** [leaving the room] I didn't come here to be insulted.
> **Malema:** Come out! Go out. Bastard! Go out. You bloody agent!
> *– Transcript of dialogue between Julius Malema and Jonah Fisher at an ANCYL news conference at Luthuli House, Johannesburg, April 2010*

Malema was born in 1983. Nelson Mandela was released when he was seven and South Africa was a fully fledged democracy when he was 11. So Malema is no struggle hero. He's a veteran of nothing but carpentry classes.

The end assumption can only be that the motivation behind Malema's hatred is power and money. Bizarrely, it is what Malema himself narrow-mindedly uses to define the "whiteness" that he seeks. He wants the nice clothes and the nice watch and the fancy cars and the house in Sandton, and he wants to exercise power for his own ends. How to do it? Mobilise the masses behind some fictional race war. Shout hate into a microphone. After all, it worked for Idi and Adolf.

Malema is, it is sad to report, acting out the archetype, playing it to a tee. In "Africa, the Post-Colonial Balls-Up", Malema is trying his darndest for a leading role. But so far he's Mugabe without the menace, Amin without the charisma. He's Bonaparte without the talent, Julius without the Caesar.

This is a man who manages to involve himself in (rather suspicious) tenders in his native Limpopo, then takes the money and fails to complete the work, impoverishing communities and the treasury, and looting hard-earned tax rands in the process. When he fails in his endeavours to win mining tenders, his reaction is not to redouble his efforts to put in better tenders; it is to demand the nationalisation of those same mines. What Juju wants, Juju will get – or he'll rage and scream about the forces aligned against him. And it doesn't matter if people must die, lose their incomes or flee the country to the detriment of us all.

Malema will support Mugabe while Zimbabweans starve. He'll encourage murder. He'll foment hatred against the former oppressor, the colonialist, the white devil, management, Cosatu, even Zuma now – whatever seems convenient at the time. He'll do whatever he needs to do, even if it means making headlines abroad and making *Time* magazine's list of 50 international morons.

I imagine Julius was a bed wetter. Perhaps he still is. His obsession with being king, his unending deep-in-the-pit-of-his-stomach yearning to be Very Important, to break free of his own smallness… It speaks volumes. My suspicion is that what's under *his* trouser is what's problematic. Once he's been and gone – for surely he will one day be gone – we'll not be measuring Malema's influence in votes or supporters, but the number of his chins and the inches on his waist.

Malema is a waddling stain on South Africa, a fine country inhabited by good people, and better than Malema in ways too myriad to mention. A book in itself. So we should take comfort from the fact that, before too long, Malema will be a mere nasty memory, just like his kindred spirit, political peer and intellectual equal, Eugène Terre'Blanche. Speak up, Julius. Shout it out! Hasten your own demise!

Where's Brutus when you need him?

(See Steve Hofmeyr and Eugène Terre'Blanche.)

Ananias Mathe

b. c 1976

Career criminal; SA's most-wanted man (November-December 2006); rapist; robber; dog killer; probable murderer; personification of South African lawlessness

WHEN, IN YEARS TO COME, the history of this time in South Africa is reviewed, it will surely be with a sense of considerable shock – something akin to the detached sadness that accompanies an account of distant horrors, such as the slaughter at the Somme, the atrocities of the Nazis or the madness in Rwanda. How else will our descendants be able to make sense of the low-level attritional war waged on the civilian population of our country in the 1990s and 2000s and, possibly, the decades to come? One can only hope that, at the very least, it causes a sharp intake of breath.

Because when we read the headlines in the morning and watch the news in the evening, surely something is wrong with the story we're being told: that 50 South Africans a day are intentionally killed at the hands of others; that Johannesburg and Cape Town regularly vie with the likes of Caracas in Venezuela and Ciudad Juárez and Tijuana in Mexico for the title of Murder Capital of the World.

Our hands are all wrung out. Our supplies of adjectives and hyperbole and indignation and rage are spent. Crime is everywhere; it's just how it is; the order of things. And this really is a war. This is what civilian populations have suffered during times of conflict from time immemorial. For comparison, consider briefly the US-led invasion of Iraq in 2003, which according to the Iraq Body Count project had caused around 105,000 civilian deaths up to October 2010. Over the same period, the South African murder rate beat that figure by something in the region of 30,000 – the ultimate pyrrhic victory.*

Oddly, it isn't a killer who has become the face of the violent criminality that's

---

* This assumes a South African murder toll of about 130,000-140,000, based on 50 deaths a day over seven-and-a-half years, and building in the declining murder rate in the last two years. Though there are far higher estimates of civilian deaths in Iraq, The Iraq Body Count project is probably the most widely cited source on the topic, and compares closely with Associated Press estimates and the Wikileaks archive that came to light in 2010.

overrun South Africa's streets, but instead a Mozambican rapist and robber. Ananias Mathe may well be a murderer, too, given the plethora of unsolved crimes in this country and the man's pathological proclivity for violent offences. But he has not been convicted for that particular crime, so it is for rape and robbery (and dog-poisoning and jail-breaking) that we know him.

He has tried to kill, of course – on several occasions, at least. When he attacked Tracy Jacobson-Goldblatt and her son in her bedroom in 2002 and she fought him off – Mathe is small and skinny – he shot her three times in the upper body. She was lucky to live, and even luckier to escape without being sexually assaulted. Other women were not so lucky.

> "He did not know how to behave in a normal society. He did not know the responsible human behaviour."
>
> *– Dr Wickus Coetzee, consulting*
> *psychologist in Mathe's 2009 criminal conviction*

Though he operated in various towns across the country from 1999, dabbling in a wide array of criminal activity, Mathe liked to concentrate his efforts in Pretoria and several Johannesburg suburbs, such as Parktown, Parkhurst and Craighall. After a while he always raped; it became his MO. Using the skills he learned from his years as a Frelimo soldier, Mathe would break in, armed with a torch and a gun. He would then rape whomever he could find in the house, be it a 70-year-old woman, or, as in one case, a 19-year-old virgin. Only then would Mathe take the car and the DVD player.

Mathe, of course, was aided by South Africa being what it is. He was arrested ten days after his (presumed) first rape but was mysteriously released. On his second arrest, for being in possession of housebreaking equipment, he absconded after paying R500 bail. In 2005, he was re-arrested, this time for rape, but he broke out of Johannesburg Central Police Station's high-risk security facility. The following year he famously escaped Pretoria's previously impregnable C-Max, most likely by bribing the guards – the story goes that his "wives" back in Mozambique raised the R80,000 required for the job. Now he's locked up again, having been found guilty on 64 counts of rape, attempted rape, attempted murder and theft.

Mathe and his criminal brethren, killers or not, take lives. They take people's futures, their hopes and their dreams, and they destroy them – because it's easy and because they assume they'll get away with it. Ultimately Mathe didn't, and he will pay the price over the next 40 or so years in C-Max, where criminals are kept in such psychologically tormenting conditions that incarceration there was described as a form of torture by the Jali Commission. It's the least he deserves.

Then again, there are so many other career criminals running free right now who deserve as much. Because South Africa is a traumatised nation. People are fleeing the carjackers and home invaders, escaping to countries where owning a car or a DVD player, or even a cellphone, is not to invite rape and murder. And every emigration impoverishes this country. Leavers take skills and money with them, and every person lost is a tiny loss of potential. The middle class is the tax base, the source of the country's potential, and Mathe and his kind are driving it away, delivering South Africa a death by a thousand cuts.

In the last two decades, Ananias Mathe and friends have turned our houses into electric-fenced prisons and our streets into dark alleyways between high walls. They've gated off neighbourhoods, etched the words "armed response" on our buildings, created countless soulless security estates and blighted the landscape with even more same-same "Tuscan" clusters. They've made South Africans angry and frightened.

But South Africans are an astonishing people. That we still get up and get on with it, that we stand together and do our best to live ordinary lives in an extraordinarily brutal time, suggests that when we are through with this all, when we finally grab our politicians' attention and convince them that, yes, we do in fact have a problem and it's time to do something about it, when we have finally reclaimed our streets, *then* we will soar.

They say the crime rate has dropped in the past few years. Just putting Ananias Mathe behind bars probably assisted with that. But there is still a long way to go until all the other Ananias Mathes out there are weeded out. Until then, we dream and wait.

Khanyi Mbau

b. 15 October 1985

Soap star; regular name on South Africa's society pages;
"Queen of Bling"; "drama queen"; "gold-digger"; "liar";
"manipulator"; "witch"

YOU KNOW, IT'S OKAY TO ADMIT IT. Khanyisile Mbau is a bit of a scorcher. History does not relate exactly how her lips and her bosom got to be the way they are, but the truth is, nonetheless, that Mbau is very, very attractive, and many red-blooded men would love to get to know her better.

But bloody hell, isn't she just a pain in the neck? Famous more for being famous than for her *Muvhango* acting career, the Johannesburg "socialite" – a euphemism if ever there was one – has veritably filled the pages of the tittle-tattle mags and rags so beloved of the vacuous since she came on the scene in 2004.

She is a woman of absolutely no substance and absolutely transparent motives. For one, that *Muvhango* role only lasted a few months before she was given the boot, allegedly for partying too much or spending all her time doing magazine shoots or a combination thereof. Then came her sugar-daddy husband, Mandla Mthembu. She was 20; he was 50. True love, she claimed. There were fights, there were break-ups, there were matching yellow Lamborghinis. Then there was the divorce when the Lambos were repossessed…

Now without an, ahem, "patron", Khanyi famously bedded a very rich, married, father-of-two businessman called Theunis Crous, also in his fifties. He described her as a "drug" and went on to have a very well-publicised affair with her. He even bought her a Lamborghini and paid the rent of her Hyde Park home.

Then, this: the final straw was when Khanyi stood over his bed in the night as he was sleeping, "speaking in tongues and performing a chilling ritual on me". He said as much in a heart-rending interview… in *You* magazine.

The thing is, like our crap soap operas, what Mbau needs to understand is that she's properly second rate. Very pretty, but still second-rate. She isn't even Paris Hilton. To start with, where's the "independent" movie? Where's the seedy sex tape?

One of the true joys of living in South Africa is that we're *not* America or the

UK. We *don't* do celebrity very well. In fact, we're blessedly rubbish at it, which is why the egregious *heat* magazine is full of pictures of Tom Cruise and "Brangelina" and the Beckhams out shopping or walking in the street. So, please, Khanyisile, leave the brainless soapies for the TV.

Thabo Mbeki

b. 18 June 1942

President of South Africa (1999-2008); chief ANC negotiator with apartheid government; struggle hero; Machiavellian political operator; nepotist; Mugabe fan; Aids and crime denialist; opportunity loser

IT'S EASY – TOO EASY – TO GET DEPRESSED about the way things are going in South Africa. It's easy to bemoan the ruling party's megalomania, its internal battles for control of budgets and tenders and its utter disregard for the average South African, considered mere disposable voting fodder. It's easy to look at the current president and wonder how such a staggeringly precipitous decline was possible. Mandela to Zuma in a few stumbling steps.

But there's another angle to all this. Isn't it remarkable that we're all still here? Isn't it a testament to the resilience and the fortitude of the people of this nation, who are among the finest the planet has to offer, that we carry on despite the worst depredations of our idiot governments?

Forget Zuma. That South Africa has survived the reign of Thabo Mbeki, the most powerful and influential man in post-apartheid South Africa, without descent into civil war is a sure sign of our hardy souls. We love this place and even a paranoid president, with the entire might of the state in his hands, could not destroy us.

Mbeki was born into the struggle, in Idutywa in the Transkei. He barely knew his father, Govan, one of the older-generation stalwarts, yet he was groomed for political stardom from an early age, appropriately educated in exile and mentored by Oliver Tambo. Perhaps surprisingly, given the aloof and uncaring reputation that he would later portray to the world, he was a charming and amiable diplomat, an important and effective negotiator in the late 1980s. Less surprisingly, he was not well liked or trusted by many within the ANC.

From virtually the day the ANC was unbanned, and probably before then, Mbeki carefully and ruthlessly plotted his assumption of power. It was said of Mbeki's political victims that they would only realise he had stabbed them in the back when they saw the knife point sticking out of their front. After Chris Hani's assassination in 1993, he comprehensively outmanoeuvred Cyril Ramaphosa, his remaining competition for deputy president, and effectively took over the running of the ANC (and then the country), with Mandela accepting his position as icon and figurehead but little more.

One needs to be exceptionally careful in criticising people who grew up fighting a dirty and dangerous war against a brutal and uncompromisingly vicious apartheid state. In a time of spies and counterintelligence, trusting the wrong person could see you dead or imprisoned. Unfortunately, Mbeki took this attitude to the extreme: he prized loyalty over probity in office as much as he had done in exile and surrounded himself with people he trusted to cover his back, as opposed to those who would do the job best. In those early years of post-apartheid democracy, Mbeki was instrumental in cultivating the insidious ANC discordance and faction fighting that would come to critically inhibit the new ruling party's ability to govern with any measure of effectiveness.

"Does HIV cause Aids? Can a virus cause a syndrome? How? It can't, because a syndrome is a group of diseases resulting from acquired immune deficiency."
– *Thabo Mbeki answering a question in parliament, September 2000*

"Nobody can show that the overwhelming majority of the 40-to-50-million South Africans think that crime is not under control. Nobody can because it's not true."
– *Thabo Mbeki speaking on SABC 2, January 2007*

"There is no crisis in Zimbabwe."
– *Thabo Mbeki speaking to reporters, as quoted by ABC News, April 2008*

A predictable and calamitous result of this way of doing business was the inexorable rise to power, and subsequent blind political protection, of such morally bankrupt individuals as Jackie Selebi, Manto Tshabalala-Msimang and Joe Modise *(see individual entries)*, each of whom would go on to forge his or her own fiefdom of shame and ill-doing to the great suffering of their country. Incompetence, self-enrichment and corruption became the order of the day, while the country was left to fend for itself. Many governmental departments achieved virtually nothing while Mbeki manoeuvred about at the top.

When the inevitable criticism of the all-powerful president and his decision making arose, he dealt with it as though his very life depended upon it. For a man who had spent half a century fighting for democracy, he wasn't terribly good at being a democrat. Dogma trumped everything, and as a result his (official) presidency was catastrophic for millions of South Africans. Regrettably, it was the poor and the voiceless who suffered most – due, among other reasons, to his disregard for the savage wave of violent crime that has hit South Africa since the mid-1990s, his stubbornly contrary views on Aids and its causes, and his apparent lack of awareness of (or concern about) the rising levels of corruption that have hindered service delivery across the land.

Mbeki refused even to recognise that crime was a problem in South Africa. He, in fact, was so incensed by newspaper reports on the topic that he was moved to hit out, dismissing offending journalists as white racists perpetuating the stereotype of black people as "barbaric savages". This despite official police statistics portraying a country in which fifty people were being murdered every day – the vast majority of them, of course, being black. Fifty people! That's an entire coach-load of mothers, fathers, brothers and sisters sent over a cliff every day. And yet the man with a hole in his soul was content merely to shoot the messenger as a white racist.

Mbeki's ability to disassociate himself from the appalling suffering of millions of people he characteristically described as "our" – that is black – people, was seemingly psychopathic. It manifested itself most tellingly in his reaction to South Africa's other grave crisis of the early democratic era: the relentless, murderous march of HIV and Aids. Again, his hard-wired mistrust of the West, of whites and of the prevailing wisdom in Western medicine would lead him to condemn many to wither away pathetically and die.

There is an image of Mbeki, a glass of hard tack to his side, sitting late into the night surfing the internet, looking for and buying into the snake-oil salesmen that would give succour to his view that the notion that HIV is sexually transmitted was yet more racist colonialist conspiracy. With HIV, as he saw it, the African was yet again being characterised by the West as a savage with little or no control over his sexual behaviour. He eloquently summarised his paranoia in a speech to students at Fort Hare University in 2001: "Convinced that we are but natural-born, promiscuous carriers of germs, unique in the world, they proclaim that our continent is doomed to an inevitable mortal end because of our unconquerable devotion to the sin of lust."

His railing against this idea would eventually lead him to deny the link between HIV and Aids, and would get him to send Tshabalala-Msimang, as health minister, to deny the thronged masses of HIV-positive poor access to the drugs that could extend and normalise their lives. Upwards of 300,000 mainly poor black people were sacrificed on the altar of Mbeki's racial paranoia. But he didn't stop there.

Notions of solidarity in all circumstances, of loyalty and of resistance to whites and to the West, all born out of a lifetime of struggle would, in arguably his greatest crime, drive Mbeki to stand by idly as an autocratic fiend of the first order destroyed an entire nation. Mbeki's support of Robert Mugabe as he systematically sacked Zimbabwe while fraudulently retaining power has had a terrible impact on South Africa that we will feel for many years, if not decades. *(See Robert Mugabe.)* Of course, its impact has been far worse in Zimbabwe, where the economy collapsed spectacularly and almost entirely in a matter of years, reducing the country to a wasteland of starving, jobless people seemingly bereft of hope.

> "Thabo Mbeki has come to represent a completely new phenomenon in black politics: he represents the end of black political morality."
>
> – *Xolela Mangcu*

Mbeki, the most powerful man in southern Africa, did nothing to stop the madness, ignoring the overwhelming and consistent complaints of democratic nations and of South African media and trade unions. Again, in all likelihood, he saw these reactions as neo-colonialist whingeing and fobbed them off with his "quiet diplomacy", a faux-intellectual front for full-on support of Mugabe. (His inaction ironically landed mortal blows to two grandly ambitious pet projects of Mbeki's: the New Partnership for African Development and the African Union.)

On the plight of the people of Zimbabwe, and the four million or more souls it would despatch to South Africa in hope of sustenance, Mbeki clearly felt nothing. And we mustn't forget to place the resulting xenophobic horrors of 2008 at Mbeki's feet. It was a final bonfire of Mbeki's vanities, but the man with a heart of pure granite refused even to speak publicly on the matter until the horrific period of violence was almost over. (Perhaps he was writing another lengthy and impenetrable ANC newsletter that the majority of South Africans could neither access nor understand.)

Mbeki also learnt from Mugabe. He, too, attempted a third term (effectively a fourth term) despite the constitutional limitation on such a notion. He, too, in his attempt to keep Zuma out of Tuynhuis, meddled calamitously with the country's legal processes. In the end, he became the African despot, the very image of Africa he accused the West, and whites, of perpetuating. Tellingly, since his departure from power he has been overlooked for two years running for the Mo Ibrahim Prize for Achievement in African Leadership. The adjudicates of that hugely lucrative (if somewhat cynical) award would apparently concur with this review of his time in office, choosing rather to award the prize to... no-one.

Mbeki symbolises the trouble that can occur when lifelong revolutionaries become politicians. He thought he was still in a war – a war with white Africans, a war with the West, a war with imperialism and colonialism. In fact he wasn't. He was running a fractious, wonderful, challenged country with very serious problems that needed fast, practical solutions. He inherited Mandela's mantle with all the opportunity and promise that it offered – and he gave us a paranoid, pipe-smoking, beard-stroking, web-browsing, perverse, disobliging mule. He gave us fifty murders a day and hundreds of thousands of premature deaths; he gave us cronyism and corruption; he gave us Zimbabwe as it is and, ultimately, despite his best efforts, he gave us Jacob Zuma.

He was so bad, in the end, that even the ANC recalled him and gave him the boot – and South Africans who had feared the rise to power of the corruption-tainted, scandal-prone, intellectually limited Zuma thought: "Hell, at least he can't be as bad as Thabo."

Lord Milner

23 March 1854 – 13 May 1925

Colonial administrator; High Commissioner for Southern Africa (1897-1905); arch Anglophile; self-confessed initiator of the Second Anglo-Boer War

IT'S A FOOL'S ERRAND TRYING TO WHAT-IF HISTORY. What if Lincoln hadn't been assassinated? Or JFK? Or Gandhi? Or Archduke Franz Ferdinand of Austria?

That last one is an interesting hypothetical, actually, because Ferdinand's death was the immediate trigger of the First World War. Together with his wife, he was shot in June 1914 in Sarajevo, Bosnia, by a young Yugoslav nationalist called Gavrilo Princip, and his death was the first domino to fall in a succession of events that led to Austria-Hungary declaring war on Serbia. After that a complex array of international alliances took effect and within weeks the major nations of the world were at war – the culmination of which in 1918/1919 laid the groundwork for the Second World War. So the Archduke's death was a decisive event in the end.*

Although it wasn't, really. Because the First World War, by that stage, was as inevitable as a war can be. Conditions were absolutely ripe for it, and Ferdinand's death was simply the starter gun going off. The athletes had been assembled and ready to go for some time.

Not all wars are inevitable, though. Rewind fifteen years to the start of the Second Anglo Boer War – or Boer War – and you have the perfect example.

The Boer War was a most tragic event in the history of South Africa, in terms of both the death and suffering it caused and its long-term ramifications, some of which, amazingly, are still felt today. It is widely considered to be the world's first "modern war", bridging as it did the 19th and 20th centuries, and pioneering

---

* The assassination itself is, in fact, a hypothetical wormhole all on its own. Ferdinand had already survived an attempt on his life earlier in the day when a bomb was thrown at his car, injuring several people. Princip, who was among the conspirators, assumed their mission a failure. But Ferdinand then chose to visit the victims of the attack in hospital later in the day. As fate would have it, the driver of his car ended up taking a wrong turn, then stalling the vehicle in the street as he tried to reverse – and Princip, gun in his pocket, just happened to be there on the side of the road. So it's possible to argue that a wrong turn and a tricky clutch "started" the First World War.

various strategies and inventions that would define conflicts to come, including camouflage, guerilla tactics, attacks on civilian targets and the widespread internment and death of civilians. Of course, the enduring notoriety of the war is due to the horrors of the concentration camps, which killed tens of thousands of noncombatants and, in particular, decimated a generation of Boer children.

It really didn't have to happen. Except that, with Lord Alfred Milner running the British show in South Africa at the time, it did.

Alfred Milner, 1ST Viscount Milner, was, like Bartle Frere before him, an Empire-smitten colonial administrator whose Anglophile convictions defined his tenure in South Africa as British High Commissioner. Indeed, on first meeting Milner, Jan Smuts described him as "a second Bartle Frere" and predicted he would be "more dangerous than Rhodes". It was an accurate assessment.

> "I think that England sinned when she got herself into a war in South Africa which she could have avoided, just as we have sinned in getting into a similar war in the Philippines."
> – *Mark Twain, comparing the Boer War to the*
> *Philippine Insurrection, also fought between 1899 and 1902*

Milner, a much-respected servant of the Empire (who would go on to serve with distinction as David Lloyd George's second-in-command during the final years of the First World War), arrived in South Africa in 1897. The ill-fated Jameson Raid into the Transvaal by a Rhodes-backed force was not much more than a year in the memory and had left its mark on the political landscape, with Paul Kruger, president of the offended republic, becoming increasingly wary in his dealings with the British. This was something of a concern given that the gold mines of the Witwatersrand were generating such fabulous wealth for their British owners. So it was a tricky diplomatic assignment that required a keen sense of empathy with the locals and a healthy level of patience. Milner had neither. He did, however, have sly cunning and a complete conviction in the rightness of empire.

There were two concerns for Milner. Firstly, the gold mines had attracted a huge influx of foreigners, or *uitlanders*, many of them subjects of the good queen Victoria, but the Boers were refusing them the vote. They were, in the parlance of the time, disenfranchised. Secondly, and more to the point, the Brits wanted to be the boss. Milner's scheme was to use the first problem to solve the second.

Over the course of 1898 and into 1899, negotiations for the Transvaal to extend more rights to British citizens bumbled along slowly and awkwardly. Kruger was understandably reluctant to hand over the vote, considering the 60,000 or more *uitlanders* now outnumbered Boers by two-to-one, but he realised concessions had to be made and he did his best to make them. Milner, though, was having none of it. He repeatedly and disingenuously rejected Boer offers, giving Kruger less and less room to manoeuvre. Though he was ultimately unable to avert Milner's agenda, the shrewd old man was well aware of what was going on; that the franchise issue was a mere ruse. "It's our country you want," he told Milner in their last meeting in June 1899. Indeed, it was.

Milner's big mistake – truly enormous in the greater scheme of things – was to underestimate what the approaching war would entail. With that consummate arrogance of Empire, he figured it would be a matter of months before Kruger's government was ousted, and he convinced Colonial Secretary Joseph Chamberlain as much. A quick victory would put the Boers in their place and deliver Britain the Transvaal, they agreed. The estimated cost of the war was put at £10 million.

In the end, the Boers made the first move in an effort to catch the British off guard and force a favourable early settlement. It was not to be, and once the imperial forces arrived en masse – 450,000 by the end of it, six times more than originally estimated – the Boers were forced to fight as guerilla units. Then came the concentration camps. The war dragged on for nearly three years and ended up costing the crown £217 million, with 22,000 British dead. About 60,000 South Africans died in total, the vast majority civilians.

At the war's end, Milner's extreme Anglo-superiority complex came to the fore once more at the negotiation table when he sought to humiliate the Boer leaders and subjugate their people. Lord Kitchener, the (hated) commander of the British forces, intervened frequently to allow for more reasonable terms at the Treaty of Vereeniging, signed in May 1902. Though Milner had miscalculated hugely and to devastating effect, he held seemingly little remorse for, in effect, starting the Boer War. He did, however, admit to the fact. "It is not very agreeable, and in many eyes not very creditable business to have been largely instrumental in bringing about a big war," he noted to Lord Roberts in 1900.

The utter futility and pointlessness of the damaging conflict was crystallised just five years after the war's end, when Britain's new Liberal leadership restored self-governance to the Boer republics, proving that a viable diplomatic solution had always existed. "They gave us back our country in everything but name," as Smuts put it. By 1910 the Union of South Africa had come into being.

So, we ask the question, what if Lord Alfred Milner had never been sent to administer the Cape Colony? What if, indeed.

(See Lord Kitchener.)

The minibus taxi driver

Visually and aurally offensive, inconsiderate, non-indicating, corner-cutting, danger-courting, stress-inducing, road-law-violating transporter of the vast majority of South Africa's blue-collar work force

IT'S EASY, IF YOU DRIVE A CAR, to blame minibus taxis. But here are some facts. Very few taxi drivers own their own taxis. Of the 200,000 or so people employed in the industry, only 20,000 own vehicles. Most work for an owner, who tells his drivers that each taxi must deliver to him R1,000 a day. Anything on top of that is the driver's pay. Hence, you see, the pressure. The pressure to get back to town to get the next load. The pressure to jam in as many passengers as possible.

Be under no illusion, a taxi driver's life is gruelling. It is seldom the drivers who can't be bothered to maintain the vehicles; it's the owners. And the owners are usually amoral, violence-inclined gangster bosses who run the entire industry – so that's more pressure to deal with, just for good measure.

Of the 40 or so people who die on South African roads every day, fewer than ten percent are killed in taxi-related accidents, illustrating that taxis are not quite the Great Satan of South African roads that we imagine them to be. But let's not get too carried away here with compassion and understanding, because taxi drivers deserve every ounce of fear and loathing we impart in their general direction.

To explain the surprising statistic above, taxis constitute less than 2 percent of the vehicles in South Africa, which is to say they cause a disproportionately large number of road deaths. The AA reckons that around 70,000 of them, equating to nearly half the country's taxi fleet, are involved in accidents every year. In other words, they do crash an awful lot and they are indeed the scum of the universe. The reason is obvious: a total disregard for traffic laws and other road users.

Here's the worst of it, though: because of minibus taxis, we have all become horrendous drivers. While taxis may be ugly and noisy, while their drivers are content to play games with the lives of 16 people at a time by running red traffic lights and driving on the wrong side of the road, while the incessant honking is infuriating and the state of the vehicles is shocking, the sad fact is that many South Africans of all kinds – rich, poor, black, white – are a disgrace on the road.

In the past few years an orange light has come to mean "floor it". Nobody knows how to use a traffic circle. Nobody wants to join a queue. Nobody wants to let anyone *into* a queue. Drivers speed irresponsibly in places where people live and children go to school. Zebra crossings are completely ignored. No-one wears a seat belt. Children sit on drivers' laps. Drivers happily block traffic if it will save them a few seconds. People who drive fancy cars or SUVs (or fancy SUVs) think they are more important than other road users… The list is endless. And it's topped by the unending propensity of South Africans to get absolutely shit-faced on a Friday night and deem that an acceptable state in which to drive home. Everyone else is doing it, right?

> "A taxi driver was arrested on Wednesday after he was caught transporting 49 schoolchildren in a 16-seater minibus taxi between KwaZulu-Natal's Mooi River and Estcourt, the Department of Transport said."
> *News report from the Mail & Guardian, 3 February 2010.*
> *The driver was found to be five times over the legal alcohol limit*

Of course, the fact that the police have decided to vigorously enforce the tiny fraction of the rules of the road that happen to be the most lucrative – speed limits – and completely ignore the rest of them, doesn't help. So we know we can cross solid lines, turn without indicating, run red robots, undertake on the hard shoulder, talk on our cellphones and all the rest, because the metro cops are eating KFC under a bush with a speed gun, or taking "rent" from unregistered taxi drivers. And so the AA's annual warning that "in almost all cases, an accident is preceded by a traffic violation" goes unheeded year after year.

Meanwhile, pedestrians are their own worst enemies, and they make up nearly half of the 40. As if in bold defiance of Darwin, many see fit to get motherless and walk along highways with nary a concern for their safety. Hence the (genuine) health warning that appears on 5-litre papsaks of wine: "Don't drink and walk on the road, you may be killed." The advice, however, remains largely ignored, and the more daring of them do it at night while wearing dark clothes.

The truth is that the aggressive Sandton mommy in her SUV shouting at taxi drivers is as bad as the taxi driver himself, and the careless pedestrian is as much a liability. We're *all* responsible for the utter stress, mayhem and carnage on South African roads. But because they are so utterly disinterested in the impact their appalling behaviour has on other people's lives, the South African bad driver has a face. And it's the sociopath behind the wheel of the HiAce. A pox upon him!

Joe Modise

23 May 1929 – 26 November 2001

Minister of Defence (1994-1999); thug; Mbeki ally; the man behind the arms deal

THERE HAVE BEEN BOOKS WRITTEN ABOUT THE ARMS DEAL. Some excellent, some rather long-winded, all considerably damning. So we're going to keep this simple. The essence of the arms deal, announced in 1999, is as follows.

Firstly, to pay for it, we diverted incredible sums of money from far worthier causes, such as healthcare, housing and energy infrastructure *(see Alec Erwin)*. As of October 2010, it had cost a reported R67 billion – which works out to around 2.2 million RDP houses.

Secondly, we got the wrong stuff. There is no credible threat to South Africa's sovereignty, now or in the foreseeable future, and certainly none that would require three diesel-electric attack submarines (costing around R5.5 billion in 1999) or four stealth frigates (also around R5.5 billion, including helicopters) to repulse. The frigates, you'd think, might at least protect our fishing rights and do a bit of patrolling, but they cost R8 million a day to run and there's no budget left over to deploy them effectively. As a result, in 2008 the navy declared it "urgently and critically" needed eight to 12 multipurpose patrol boats, at around R300 million each. Then we have our 26 new JAS 39 Gripen fighters, which are exceptionally cool, but are short-range single-engine planes built for northern-European conditions. More to the point, we only have nine pilots (and one navigator) capable of flying them as of November 2010 and, like the navy, we can barely afford to run them. Also, fighter jets don't provide a peacekeeping role, so the air force subsequently had to order hugely expensive heavy-lift transport planes for this purpose (a separate controversy altogether). And that's just a taster of that aspect of the deal.

Thirdly, the reason we diverted incredible sums of money from far worthier projects and the reason we got the wrong stuff is because the entire process was born of corruption, bribery and back-door shenanigans.

As every South African knows, there has never been a comprehensive parliamentary enquiry into the arms deal, despite constant requests from the public, opposition leaders, Cosatu, the British government and various other interested parties. On the one hand, this is an astounding realisation, given the sheer weight of evidence pointing to widespread bribery and corruption at virtually every level of the procurement process. Britain's Serious Fraud Office (SFO), for example, believes that R1 billion in illegal "commissions" was paid by BAE Systems to facilitate deals – and they just provided the jets. On the other hand, the decision to not investigate is not surprising at all: there are just too many big names who could take a fall – from Mbeki and Zuma down through government to all the various influential businessmen and companies involved – and there has, evidently, been too much pressure from too many directions to allow it to happen. In October 2010 the Hawks officially closed down their investigation.

> "Modise was transparently intent on using his tenure at the Ministry of Defence as a springboard to becoming seriously rich, showing almost no interest in doing his ministerial job. He would not even read departmental or cabinet papers, left the job of integrating the old South African Defence Force and MK into the new South African National Defence Force to his deputy, Ronnie Kasrils, and concentrated entirely on the arms deal."
> – *Extract from South Africa's Brave New World by RW Johnson*

Without some kind of official enquiry, it will be impossible to say for sure who did what and who got what out of the arms deal. And even if there were one, it would doubtless be dreadfully politicised. So we're just going to take all the allegations and evidence out there and dump the blame for this gargantuan political, socioeconomic and military debacle onto the head of Joe Modise.

You may recall Johannes "Bra Joe" Modise as the minister of defence who presided over that little foray into Lesotho when the South African National Defence Force couldn't read a map right and got into a spot of bother while trying to prevent a coup in that country. It was a rather embarrassing affair all round. But Modise was a lot more than a debacle in Lesotho.

A truck driver and gangster in 1950s Alexandra, he is recalled as a rather bad bugger by veterans of the struggle. As a founding member and then commander of Umkhonto we Sizwe, he came with a serious reputation. "Everyone in the ANC was frightened of him," Sibusiso Madlala, a senior MK operative, explained in an interview with historian RW Johnson. "They knew he had killed people himself, that he was completely ruthless and that he had presided over mass torture and executions in the MK punishment camps." On top of this, he was widely held to be an informer for the apartheid government, and he was later suspected of playing a role in the murder of Chris Hani, a rival of his and of his ally, Thabo Mbeki.

In the transition to ANC rule, Modise played an important and early role in negotiations, and he shrewdly and deliberately positioned himself to become South Africa's first black defence minister, a position that would offer plenty of opportunity for self-enrichment. Modise had shown great support in getting Mbeki into the position of Mandela's heir apparent, and Mbeki repaid the favour by letting him do pretty much as he wanted in the Ministry of Defence – and that meant cashing in on the upcoming arms deal, despite objections from the likes of Jay Naidoo, Joe Slovo and Trevor Manuel.

Modise was involved in all aspects of the arms deal. Among other things, he intervened in the contract for light fighter trainers, ensuring BAE Hawks were selected rather than the cheaper Italian alternative. One of the principal beneficiaries of this deal, according to the SFO, was Fana Hlongwane, Modise's friend and adviser, who they say pocketed £3 million. Indeed, it was later observed that Modise's close friends "seemed to be men who had profited from the arms deal". His daughter even found her way onto the board of one of the companies designated for counter-trade agreements. And when he stood down as defence minister in 1999, he himself joined the boards of several companies that had benefited. All in, Modise is said to have received more than R10 million in arms-deal "commissions", according to Andrew Feinstein, author of *After The Party*.

No-one is claiming that corruption didn't exist before the arms deal or before 1994. Indeed, the story goes that the first thing the Nats did when handing over the country to the ANC was ensure they were all set up with nice beach houses and game concessions to retire to. But the arms deal stands as a crucial landmark on South Africa's post-democracy path: the moment when so many ANC freedom fighters who had defined themselves in the collective drive for the liberation of South Africa and a better life for all decided it was time to change focus and look out for number one. It was the biggest post-democratic gravy train of them all and, with Modise as its chief conductor, it proved to be unstoppable.

As a final illustrative vignette, consider the fate of Tony Yengeni, the only politician to have been convicted for taking a bribe related to the arms deal, a discount on a Mercedes-Benz, which saw him serve five months of a four-year sentence. Problem is, the company that admitted it "rendered assistance" in getting him his new wheels, the European Aeronautic Defence and Space Company, admits it did the same for thirty senior government officials. Thirty!

Whether they actively profited from the arms deal or they just watched their friends and colleagues do so, the new rulers of South Africa had quickly learnt what it meant to cash in at the expense of their fellow countrymen. And, for leading by example, we have Joe Modise to thank for this.

Patrice Motsepe

b. 28 January 1962

South Africa's richest individual; nice guy; archetypal
example of the failed implementation of BEE

FORBES RATES HIM THE 421ST RICHEST PERSON on the planet, yet he doesn't go in for show. He's just got the one house (a nice one, admittedly, in the posh Johannesburg suburb of Bryanston), there's no yacht or fleet of luxury supercars or any of the usual follies that billionaires can get themselves mixed up with. Indeed his only weakness, it seems, is for football, which is why he is owner and chairman of Mamelodi Sundowns. He's Patrice Motsepe, and he's well known to be a decent enough bloke. But he's far, far too rich.

Motsepe's massive wealth is the product of good intentions badly executed. Most sane people understand the need to drive black ownership and involvement in the formal economy in modern South Africa. So it's not the fundamental idea behind Black Economic Empowerment – or Broad-Based Black Economic Empowerment, if we must – that's problematic. It's just that the law as it stands is not working. Because replacing one tiny elite with another isn't broad-based anything. It's just bollocks. Or, as Jeremy Cronin asks, "At what point does a black multimillionaire cease to be historically disadvantaged?"

Motsepe, of course, is not the problem here; he's the symptom. And his story is, at least, a good one. He grew up poor, worked hard and excelled at school (in Aliwal North), eventually managing to persuade various apartheid minions to let him study at Wits University. He went on to work at Bowman Gilfillan, one of the country's biggest corporate law firms, where he was something of a star. He became the company's first black partner in 1994.

But the lure of BEE was too promising to pass over so, shortly after, Motsepe established his own enterprise, a contract-mining firm called Future Mining, just as laws were being implemented to force companies to not only incorporate black ownership but also black contractors. In 1997 he started African Rainbow Minerals, and before too long he was flying. Now he's a BEE partner to Harmony Gold and, weirdly, Sanlam, of which he will eventually own ten percent. He has become stunningly rich and a household name.

To be fair to Motsepe he's only on these pages because he's on top of the BEE pile, the richest of the lot. You can replace him with Tokyo Sexwale or Cyril Ramaphosa or Lazarus Zim if you wish. And, of course, extreme wealth isn't a crime. But extreme poverty is, and that's what South Africa's empowerment laws ought to address. In the case of Motsepe, a few very rich white people have been replaced with one colossally rich black person. If there are 40 million black people in South Africa, a great many of whom are devastatingly poor, then you might argue that, in Patrice Motsepe, the implementation of BEE as it works today has solved one 40-millionth of our problem. Add Sexwale, Ramaphosa, Zim and maybe Phuthuma Nhleko or Sipho Nkosi to the list, and suddenly five 40-millionths are solved... Way to go, BEE.

"Our peculiar version of Black Economic Empowerment has raged on despite severe criticism from all sectors of society – apart from white capitalists, the few black beneficiaries and the ANC leadership, of course."

– *Max du Preez*

Incidentally – or, perhaps, not so incidentally – Motsepe's sister Bridgette is herself a stinking rich mining boss. Handily, she's married to Justice Minister Jeff Radebe. And in November 2010, Patrice Motsepe agreed to donate R10 million to the Jacob Zuma Foundation because, he said, he believes it is important to share what he had with the poor. You see what he did there?

Politics and money are seldom too far apart in South Africa, but R10 million is not really all that much money for Motsepe, who the *Sunday Times* estimated to be worth more than R14.2 billion in 2009. Indeed, you might call it a very astutely spent bagatelle.

Motsepe is on record saying that he's received no hand-outs and has worked very hard for his money. This is probably true. It's also exactly the same cry white South Africans make about their own wealth. Of course you worked hard for it. Nobody denies it. But did not the law favour you unfairly? That the gap between the rich and the poor in this country is ever wider, that we are now considered the most unequal society in the world, is a damning indictment on the failure of BEE policies to broaden the base of wealth.

The law needs to be revisited. It's not working for the poor. But it is working for the very rich and their political chums – so don't hold your breath.

Robert Mugabe

b. 21 February 1924

Prime Minister of Zimbabwe; genocidal despot; economy ruiner; country pillager; specific cause of Zimbabwean exodus to South Africa and resulting socioeconomic disaster

IT'S ODD, ISN'T IT, THAT THE LEADER of an independent African nation, and a man who was instrumental in shedding the yoke of minority white rule, would find himself starring in a book about people who did their best to stuff up South Africa? But, if you think about it, Robert Mugabe really has done a number on us. It's not that he's stolen our resources or invaded us or anything – except that, in a sense, that's exactly what he's done.

Mugabe, let's be clear, is a choice-grade dictator and has, after thirty years in charge, earned himself a spot on Africa's Top Ten Best Dictators Ever list. And yet for years Zimbabwe was a peaceful and relatively prosperous place, with Mugabe presiding over the best education system in Africa, a hugely productive agricultural sector and a thriving tourism industry. Any South African who visited Zimbabwe in the 1990s, as our local murder rate soared, found it to be a peaceful, happy place inhabited by genuinely pleasant people and blessed with some of the most beautiful countryside ever bequeathed on a nation by God.

Of course, that peace had come at huge cost. Mugabe and his Zanu and Zapu colleagues had fought a vicious and brutal bush war against Ian Smith's Rhodesia, in which not just the army but also farmers found themselves on the front line. Mugabe eventually took power in 1980. Those first years were a wobbly time for his country, with the largely Shona Zanu butting heads with the largely Ndebele Zapu, headed by Joshua Nkomo. By 1982 it seemed that a state of civil war was imminent, but Mugabe dealt with the problem in characteristic fashion.

Back in 1980 he had asked his chum Kim Il Sung of North Korea to help train a crack brigade of Zimbabwean troops, and Kim had despatched more than 100 of his soldiers to do just that. They were to become the Fifth Brigade, known as the Gukurahundi, and they reported directly to the prime minister – namely, Mugabe. Come the tensions of 1982 and the Fifth Brigade was ordered to Matabeleland, whereupon a typically nasty bout of African genocide ensued. Some say as many as 20,000 Ndebele, mainly civilians, were executed, rounded up into huts and burnt to death or just shot out of hand. Bodies were often dumped down unused mine shafts. By the end of it Mugabe, a Shona, had used a ruthless modern-day army to get even with none other than Mzilikazi *(see Shaka)*. With Nkomo and the Ndebele quelled, and with the later merger of Zanu and Zapu into Zanu-PF, Mugabe's hold on power was absolute. And he had no plans to relinquish it.

"We have nothing to show for our independence, except overwhelming poverty."

– Morgan Tsvangirai, April 2006

"We are not going to give up our country because of a mere X. How can a ballpoint pen fight with a gun?"

– Robert Mugabe, June 2008

Relative calm prevailed until 1997, when a change of government in the UK saw Tony Blair's new Labour Party come to power. They took a look at their finances and made the decision to stop funding Mugabe's land-reform process, mainly because the money was being used to buy farms for him and his chums. Mugabe reacted to this by abandoning the "willing buyer, willing seller" arrangement that had ultimately failed to see the 70 percent of farmland that was owned by whites transferred into black hands. Then, in 2000, Mugabe suffered a humiliating blow when Zimbabweans voted against his plan to make amendments to the country's constitution for a variety of self-serving reasons. It was downhill from there.

With his grasp on power slipping, Mugabe needed to do something extreme, so he went with the base appeal to populism by having his "war veteran" henchmen start violently evicting white farmers from their land. The historical context to this is all quite obvious *(see Cecil John Rhodes)*, but in the process Mugabe showed the world that property rights no longer existed in Zimbabwe. Businesses packed up and left. Tourists stopped coming. Farms lay ruined and unproductive as their new "owners" left them to rot. The formal economy fell apart as hyperinflation set in, topping out at an incomprehensible 500-billion percent, before the Zim dollar was scrapped in 2008.

Meanwhile, Mugabe utterly sacked the country's institutions, the courts, the constitution and any semblance of civilisation. Elections were rigged and the horrors of the Gukurahundi revisited, with widespread violence and intimidation.

At the end of it all – today – Zimbabwe is ruined. As it has been so famously said: from bread basked to basket case in just one decade. Or as one commentator phrased it, "In today's Zimbabwe, once one of Africa's most developed states with its best-educated populace, the question is often asked, 'what did we have before candles?': the answer is, 'electricity.'"

Of course, the result has been depopulation. Those who could get out, did, even if that meant bribing a South African border official. Many went to Britain, but the most, as many as five million, came to South Africa, the majority of them illegally.

It hardly needs to be said that South Africa's response to the Zimbabwe crisis has been pathetic. President Mbeki spoke of "quiet diplomacy" to handle the situation, but in fact he simply propped up the butcher to our north by giving him the fuel of legitimacy to continue destroying his country. Even after the Movement for Democratic Change's widely acknowledged 2008 election victory, he literally held Mugabe's hand as the dictator clung to power. In the process he did immense damage to South Africa's international reputation and to the world's general sense of goodwill towards us. *(See Thabo Mbeki.)*

But, for South Africa, it has meant far more than a tarnished name. With four to five million refugees fleeing to our townships and squatter camps, large-scale socioeconomic problems were inevitable. Many were (and still are) desperate and poor, and South Africa simply doesn't have the infrastructure to handle such an influx. We don't have enough hospitals, schools, houses or jobs. And that last one is the real stinker. Probably South Africa's greatest challenge is our debilitating (official) 25 percent unemployment rate – the root cause of so many of our concerns – and yet here we are expanding our potential workforce at a rate of knots. It's simply not sustainable, and the inevitable friction that has shamefully manifested itself as "xenophobic" violence, most notably in 2008, is merely a symptom of this problem.

So this is how Robert Gabriel Mugabe has helped to stuff us up. That, and the fact that his ruined country sits as a spectre – a blueprint, if you like – of how relatively happy days can turn to murderous anarchy so very, very quickly. Robert Mugabe, in rather good English, has written the manual. Best we burn it.

Essop Pahad

b. 21 June 1939

Minister in the Presidency (1999-2008); "Mbeki's Rottweiler"; a vision of media censorship to come?

WHY WAS ESSOP PAHAD SO INCREDIBLY UNLIKABLE in his role as minister in the presidency for all those years? The probable answer is that he, like his boss Thabo Mbeki, never really got out of the trenches of a war he'd already won. He is, after all, an activist and politician who played an admirable role in the liberation of South Africa, but one wonders if he still goes to bed at night dreaming, like a shell-shocked veteran of Delville Wood, of the bloody battles of the past.

After becoming politically active as a teenager in the late 1950s, when he joined the Transvaal Indian Youth Congress and then the ANC, Pahad was arrested by the security police in 1962. There followed a long life in exile, with Pahad moving to the UK, where he gained a PhD in history at the University of Sussex. As it happened, there was another exiled young South African doing his studies at this particular institute at the time: Thabo Mbeki.

On his return home, Pahad stuck close to Mbeki who, as we've seen, prized loyalty. Pahad was happy to play the role of gatekeeper, serving as his parliamentary counsellor during the deputy presidency before being rewarded as minister in the presidency after the 1999 election that saw Mbeki's installation in Tuynhuis.

It is in this role that Pahad served as what Graeme Addison would call "an intellectual bouncer at the president's club, fond of hurling abuse at the media". As Mbeki's presidency thundered on, increasingly disastrously, Pahad became more and more irascible in his dealings not only with the media, but also with the ANC's own MPs. He was the unquestioning servant, the overzealous PR, who would have defended Mbeki to the hilt if he'd declared the moon to be made of cheese – which he pretty much did during the prolonged HIV/Aids fiasco. Pahad pumped the president's line come what may, and those who crossed it felt the full force of the "Rottweiler in the presidency". With something of a Lurch look about him, he seemed always on the verge of using physical force to get his way.

He would rail against journalists, newspapers and anyone who questioned his boss. When the *Sunday Times* ran an incendiary story about then-Health Minister

Manto Tshabalala-Msimang's behaviour in hospital, he called for a government boycott of the paper. *(See Manto Tshabalala-Msimang.)* When the same paper reported on troublesome allegations of bribery against Mbeki, he threatened to sue. He was widely feared and despised by parliamentary reporters.

When Mbeki was sacked as president by the ANC in 2008, Pahad, loyal to the end, resigned in support. Tongue embedded firmly in cheek, this is how then-*Times* editor Ray Hartley "wept" at the news: "Who will convene summits of government and media leaders in which lecturing, hectoring and threats will be used to try and undermine the independence of so-called editors in the name of so-called freedom of expression?"

Pahad very clearly believed that the media were out to get Mbeki, so much so that he now edits his own magazine, somewhat preposterously titled *The Thinker*. His talents as an editor can perhaps be best expressed in its audited sales figures. The second quarter of 2010 stands as a good example: just over 5,000 copies on average were printed per month, of which 809 were sold, 1,095 were given away and 3,098 were returned. A little embarrassing, you'd think, but Pahad is nothing if not committed to his line of thinking.

He is also heavily involved with the nascent *New Age*, a newspaper that will have a pro-ANC editorial view and, like *The Thinker*, is funded by Jacob Zuma-aligned businessman Atul Gupta. Finally, South Africa has a newspaper that doesn't criticise the ANC-led government...

But what, one wonders in all of this, would motivate the established South African media to go after the ANC's bigwigs in the first place? Could it be the interest of the country? No! It was race, of course. Like Mbeki, Pahad was fighting what he quite probably saw as a "white" media. And, while racism and incompetence are sure to be found in South African newspapers – and newspapers across the world – the notion of there being some kind of organised assault was pure paranoia.

But on he went. Extremist whites, said Pahad, were responsible for fomenting the "xenophobia" of 2008, not Mbeki's policies on Zimbabwe. He also railed against whites, who wanted, he said, the Soccer World Cup to be a failure. This despite a Human Sciences Research Council paper that established the very opposite. It never stopped.

Pahad, in the end, went to his political grave uninterested in the truth, and only concerned with the victory of the ANC, and particularly Mbeki, in any matter and at whatever cost. In many ways, it is his "party-first people-second" approach that paved the way for a political landscape that can now countenance the looming Protection of Information Bill and Media Appeals Tribunal. Quite the legacy.

(See Thabo Mbeki.)

Kevin Pietersen

b. 27 June 1980

SA-born English cricketer; record-breaking batsman;
ex-captain of England; egomaniac; traitor; twat

Isn't Kevin Pietersen just the biggest douchebag on the planet? Not to put too crude a spin on the man, but if you're a South African reading this and you know your cricket then you can only be nodding your head right now. Not only is he supremely, supremely arrogant and a veritable walking cliché of risible football-star-type behaviours – the look-at-me body stylings, the pop-star wife, the public outbursts, the autobiography after barely a year's worth of international experience – but, well, he's a big fat traitor.

Before we get into all that, though, let's try divorcing ourselves from the subject for a moment, and look at Pietersen from the point of view of someone who's not South African. There certainly is a lot to admire about Kevin Pietersen the cricketer. It's a mug's game comparing modern players with those from the past, but his record is comparable with the best.

In his first 25 Tests, Pietersen scored 2,448 runs, a figure bettered only by that statistical hiccup known as Donald Bradman. Towards the end of a rough 2010 he was still averaging around 48, and had scored more than 5,300 runs in 66 matches. He may not be the loveliest batsman to watch, but he sure makes for compelling viewing when he's on fire. In his pomp, cutting loose, there really are shades of Everton Weekes, Viv Richards and Sunil Gavaskar about him. He's got a devastating drive and is lethal on the hook too. He fairly invented the preposterously flamboyant switch-hit, a shot so difficult that virtually no-one else attempts it, and the "flamingo" shot, a wristy flick played while hopping into the air, is all his too.

So he's good, then. World class. And like it or not, South Africans will never be able to take that fact away from Pietersen. Or KP, as the English public affectionately call him – or Kapers as his team-mates know him – or Figjam, as the Aussies refer to him. As in "Fuck I'm good, just ask me".

Which brings us back to the other thing: Kevin Pietersen, the man.

Pietersen was born in Pietermaritzburg and attended Maritzburg College. In other words, he's South African. But unlike most talented and aspiring young South African sportsmen out there, his greatest dream was not to represent his country at international level; it was – if his actions are anything to go by – to be rich and famous. South Africa be damned.

At the age of 20, Pietersen left to play first-class cricket in England after struggling to get regular game time for the Natal Dolphins. The story, as he tells it, went that quota regulations stipulating that four players in the starting line-up had to be non-white were holding back his career. So when Clive Rice offered him a contract at Nottinghamshire, where he could qualify as a local player due to his British passport and get guaranteed playing time, he took the opportunity and left.

That in itself is not Pietersen's crime – nothing wrong with getting some overseas experience under the belt as a young player. Rather, it was the way he resentfully turned his back on his country right then and there, supposedly because of quota-selection difficulties, when he was, in fact, averaging just 20 or so with the bat and about 30 with the ball. (He was an off-spinner who batted a bit in those days.) Here was this unknown youngster, barely out of his teens, and with such staggering arrogance already that he demanded a first-team spot while not really doing that much to warrant it.

Then, having played abroad and established himself as a top-class prospect, he chose not to return home to play for the Proteas, as he undoubtedly could have. Rather, he found he'd taken a liking to the lifestyle that the Poms and their precious pounds were offering up, so he figured he'd prefer to represent England – England, for crying out loud! – over South Africa. Already this is enough to shake your head at with scornful dismay. How shallow a character to willfully forsake your country… But wait – because just like a bad infomercial (in which Pietersen would no doubt appear, if the money was right) – there's more!

The topper – the fact that ensured Pietersen's name in infamy – was his juvenile decision to attack South Africa while justifying his decision to leave rather than just manning up to the fact that he was a hugely self-involved cricketing mercenary. Since his first international tour to South Africa, he's been permanently on the offensive, getting all huffy about how tough the quota systems had made his life, implying that his country abandoned him and not the other way around. No-one's buying that, though. Yes, quotas have always been a divisive and contentious problem to surmount (see *The guy I sat next to at the polo*), but they hardly stopped the likes of Graeme Smith, AB de Villiers and Dale Steyn from getting to the top. Pietersen would have walked into the South African side in due time.

It has come as no surprise to cricket-loving South Africans to learn, over the years, just how unlikable Pietersen is in person. He falls out with everybody. First there was Natal. Then came Notts, where he clashed with the management once Clive Rice departed, and famously had his kitbag thrown off the Trent Bridge balcony by Jason Gallian, the Notts captain (and subsequent hero in South African cricketing circles). More recently he even managed to fall out with Hampshire, where there had been relative calm (probably because he hardly played a game in his five years with the county due to his commitments to England). But his most famous fallout was with England coach Peter Moores, which cost him his England captaincy after just five months and, arguably, led to his current lack of form – a lack of form that saw him dropped from the England ODI side in 2010 for the first time, resulting in an ego-fantastic Twitter outburst bemoaning his dire treatment at the hands of the selectors. And we're right back where we started.

> "I'm patriotic about my country, and that's why I don't like Kevin Pietersen. The only reason that Kevin and I have never had a relationship is because he slated South Africa. It was his decision to leave and that's fine, but why does he spend so much time slating our country?"
>
> *– Graeme Smith, South African cricket captain*

Which all begs the question: was it really quotas that sent him packing from Natal in the first place? Or was it just a handy excuse when he realised that no-one there liked him?

Pietersen, with his ridiculously affected half-Estuary-half-Maritzburg accent, his insistence on kissing the three lions and all the rest of it, is famously "charmless", to quote *The Guardian*. Even in England the Ashes hero is not exactly the people's favourite and could never reach the cult-hero status of the likes of Andrew Flintoff or even Graeme Swann. Pietersen will never be loved, something former England captain Michael Vaughan says hurts him the most. For unimpressed South Africans there's some succour there.

But the conclusion that Pietersen is, indeed, a universally acknowledged twat doesn't necessarily justify his spot on a list of people who've stuffed up South Africa. So why's he here? Is he *that* big a twat that he's actually forged a new image in the UK of the insufferable South African egomaniac? No, not really. The Poms are smart enough to realise he's a special case; and, besides, these days he fits right in alongside their reality-TV stars and football celebs. He has, however, started a worrying trend.

Many South African-born players have represented the English cricket team. Including Pietersen, four have even captained the side. But they have always tended to do it for reasons of practicality: sports boycotts, actual emigration, that kind of thing. Now, Pietersen has made it acceptable to do it because the pay's better, the competition softer. Hence we've recently lost the talented young wicket-keeper batsman Craig Kieswetter to the dark side, despite concerted efforts to lure him into the Proteas' system. In this dilemma is the potential ruination of South African cricket.

More than that, though, Pietersen should have had a decade-long career in South African colours. We've done well in that time; better than England, at least. But Pietersen might have added that vital extra element of world-class performance that entrenched the Proteas at the top of the rankings, rather than the irregular moments of glory we've enjoyed. Hey, he may be a giant idiot – but when a giant idiot is *your* giant idiot, you can at least live with that. Which is why André Nel isn't in this book.

Andries Pretorius

27 November 1798 – 23 July 1853

*Boer leader during and after the Great Trek; victorious
commander at the Battle of Blood River; cementer of
Boer-Zulu antagonism by way of divine justification*

THIS ONE COULD WELL GO TO BOER LEADER PIET RETIEF because in a sense he
started it all. By imperiously expecting Dingane to grant him and his people land
rights once they'd trekked into Zululand in 1837, despite warnings that this was a
most unlikely outcome, he in effect created the conditions for his brutal murder
and the bloodshed and enmity to come. His less-than-diplomatic negotiations – in
which Dingane was offered veiled threats of what might happen should the Boers
be displeased with his conduct – aggravated the Zulu king's insecurity and led to
his ill-considered and foolhardy decision to "kill the wizards" and massacre all of
Retief's followers. *(See Dingane.)*

But this isn't chaos theory. In a pragmatic reading of history, the family tree of
cause and effect is only so big. And besides, Retief had at least publicly declared,
before setting out on his trek from his farm in the Winterberg District, that he
wished to live in peace with the native chiefdoms his people might encounter.

Truth be told, there were a variety of pertinent factors that led to the Boers'
conflict with the Zulus; in hindsight it appears to have been an inevitability. But
Andries Pretorius qualifies on these pages as the cementer of their long-standing
antagonism if only because of his decision to compare his followers to the chosen
people of Israel and to lay the fate of his vengeance of Retief's death and the
Weenen and Blaauwkrantz massacres in the hands of God.

Pretorius's defeat of Dingane's army at Blood River was certainly well executed,
but any number of Boer commanders could have done the same. The rifles and
cannons pretty much gave them the edge. But in making his Biblical parallel,
in which Natal was deemed the Boer's Promised Land just as the Israelites had
been granted Canaan, Pretorius managed to entrench in the collective Boer (and
eventually Afrikaner) consciousness the belief that their subjugation of the Zulus
was the Lord's will.

In particular, the Afrikaner nation would go on to celebrate the day as

Geloftedag, or the Day of the Vow, after a pact the trekkers had made with God about a week before the battle. Give us victory, they had prayed, and we shall build a church in Your honour. (The church still exists: it's in Pietermaritzburg, as part of the excellent Voortrekker Museum.) Various details surrounding the covenant have become disputed over time; for one, it is believed that very few of the 470 Boer fighters involved in the battle, including Pretorius himself, actually upheld the promise of celebrating the day as sacred in the years that followed. But the "official" version of the events that day would later claim that the Boers' descendants were bound by the vow to celebrate the date as a religious holiday, and in 1880 Paul Kruger encouraged commemoration of the date as Dingane's Day. Upon union in 1910, the first South African government declared it a public holiday. Later, in 1952, its name was changed to the Day of the Vow.

"Here we stand before the holy God of heaven and earth, to make a vow to Him that, if He will protect us and give our enemy into our hand, we shall keep this day and date every year as a day of thanksgiving like a sabbath, and that we shall erect a house to His honour wherever it should please Him, and that we also will tell our children that they should share in that with us in memory for future generations. For the honour of His name will be glorified by giving Him the fame and honour for the victory."

– Wording of the vow believed to be from a reconstruction by GBA Gerdener in his 1919 biography of Sarel Cilliers, the spiritual leader of Pretorius's trek group. No record of the original exists

Pretorius proved to be an able and key leader for the Boers over a decade and a half, and is generally regarded as one of the greatest of the Trek leaders. Pretoria is named for him. But it has been plausibly argued that the legend of the vow, which he created, ultimately served as divine affirmation among the Afrikaner population of white superiority over black Africans, and as a "mythological legitimisation of Afrikaner nationalism and its apartheid manifestation in the 20th century". In 1938 DF Malan declared in a speech at the site of the battle that its soil was "sacred", noting that it was "here that the future of South Africa as a civilised Christian country and the continued existence of the responsible authority of the white race was decided". *(See DF Malan.)*

As of 1994, the once-divisive date of 16 December has been observed on the South African calendar as the Day of Reconciliation. It sure took long enough to get there.

Cecil John Rhodes

5 July 1853 – 26 March 1902

Prime Minister of the Cape Colony (1890-1896);
founder of De Beers; monopolist; racist; empire builder;
megalomaniac; key player in the instigation of the
Second Anglo-Boer War; user and corrupter of people

THEY SAY, ONLY HALF-JOKINGLY, that the British climate was the greatest ever colonising force in the history of the world. In one case, certainly, it would appear to be the truth. It was the English weather that despatched, in 1870, one of the most successful and voracious colonialists in African and world history to Natal where, his parents hoped, the hot climate would help him deal with his asthma and weak heart and lungs. Cecil John Rhodes's father was a minister, and his decision to send his teenaged son to his elder brother Herbert's cotton farm in the Umkomazi Valley would have tremendous implications for the subcontinent that are very much felt today.

Rhodes's immense and enduring influence from Cape Town to Lake Tanganyika was possible because of the confluence of two vitally important factors: his enormous fortune, gained at such an early age; and his fervent belief in the rightness and necessity of English imperialism.

Rhodes's initial wealth came from his dealings on the diamond mines in Kimberley. With fabulous rags-to-riches tales of diamond discovery doing the rounds throughout the Natal colony, Herbert had forsaken his cotton venture not long after his brother's arrival and headed to the Griqualand. A year later, the sickly young Rhodes, aged only 18, followed him there, walking a substantial length of the 650-kilometre route after his horse had died. The journey took him more than a month, a fitting introduction to the hard living ahead.

A motivated and street-smart operator, Rhodes got his hands dirty, literally. He dug for diamonds. He sold ice cream on the hot streets. He networked and planned and collaborated, and he proved to be a brilliant, if ruthless, businessman. In the early 1870s the mines faced a terrible depression when it became increasingly difficult to extract diamonds from the notorious blue ground that diggers were finding beneath the softer yellow earth. Rhodes, still a relatively small operator, gobbled up claims from desperate claim owners on the De Beers mine. At one-fifth of the value of the Kimberley mine, De Beers was considered a poorer option, but Rhodes's strategy would pay off soon enough.

Conditions in the open-cast mines were extremely tough. With various claims digging at differing speeds, collapses were common and flooding a constant challenge. For workers in the pits it was a grim and dangerous existence. The shallower De Beers, however, turned out to be cheaper to dig than Kimberley and was less prone to disaster. As Rhodes consolidated, so the money poured in.

With invaluable assistance from Alfred Beit, he had by 1888 cajoled, bullied and persuaded the major industry players, including one Barney Barnato, that Kimberley's diamond mines ought to be controlled by a single entity. In the final negotiations it is said that Barnato conceded to Rhodes with the words, "Some people have a fancy for *this* thing and some for *that*. You have a fancy for empire. Well, I suppose I must give it to you." De Beers Consolidated Mines was formed in March of that year, with Rhodes declaring his intent to make it "the richest, the greatest, and the most powerful company the world has ever seen". He was despised by the many poor miners he had put out of work but, at the age of 35, he was in today's terms a billionaire.

"Money is power, and what can one accomplish without power? That is why I must have money. Ideas are no good without money... For its own sake I do not care for money. I never tried it for its own sake but it is a power and I like power."

– *Cecil John Rhodes*

By September of 1889, De Beers had a monopoly on all of Kimberley's mines, its control of the international market was complete and it was indeed one of the most powerful companies in the world; a vision of the soulless corporate future had emerged from the soil and dust of the Griqualand. Even today, 120 years later, De Beers maintains a mafia-like grip on the international trade in diamonds.

Extreme capitalism was, however, not destined to be Rhodes's greatest offence – because it had never been about the money. Far from it. Money was simply a means.

It took him a while, due to his burgeoning mining interests, but Rhodes found time to take regular boat trips back to England to study at Oriel College, Oxford, a place that impressed him greatly. He was much affected by the teachings of John Ruskin, who exhorted his undergraduates thus: "We are still undegenerate in race;

a race mingled with the best northern blood... Will you youths of England make your country again a royal throne of kings, a sceptred isle? This is what England must either do or perish; she must found colonies as fast and as far as she is able, formed of her most energetic and worthiest men; seizing every piece of fruitful waste ground she can set her foot on, and there teaching these her colonists that their chief virtue is to bear fidelity to their country, and that their first aim is to advance the power of England by land and sea."

So inspired, Rhodes developed some powerful racial notions about the possible destiny of the English while at Oxford. "Why should we not form a secret society with but one object, the furtherance of the British Empire and the bringing of the whole world under British rule, for the recovery of the United States, for making the Anglo-Saxon race but one Empire? What a dream, but yet it is probable, it is possible," he wrote. A political career beckoned.

In 1881, with his mines thriving, the 28-year-old Rhodes was elected to the Cape Colony parliament, where he noted that "Africa is still lying ready for us. It is our duty to take it." Six years later, his methods were articulated when he observed that "the native is to be treated as a child and denied the franchise. We must adopt a system of despotism in our relations with the barbarians of South Africa."

Around this time, Rhodes played a key role in the development of barracks-style housing for black mine workers, effectively paving the way for the destructive migrant-labour system to be enforced as the way to do business across South Africa in the century to come. It was a system that was to encourage chronic worker abuse and exploitation, and created the perfect breeding ground for future social dysfunction and political violence. In November 2010, the Centre for the Study of Violence and Reconciliation identified social behaviour inculcated on South Africa's mines as a critical contributing factor to the brutal nature of crime in the country today.

By 1891 Rhodes was prime minster of the Cape Colony. He had also established the British South Africa Company (BSAC), a chartered company much like the Dutch East India Company (see Jan van Riebeeck), which had an astonishing mandate to exert British influence over vast expanses of the African interior, and could call on its own private army to do so. On top of this, Rhodes controlled 90 percent of the world's diamond production.

As prime minister, he – naturally – pursued legislation that favoured mine owners, such as laws that allowed the government to boot black people off their land to allow for such developments, as well as the hated "hut tax". As head of the BSAC he would pursue wildly ambitious and massively damaging colonising adventures in the name of a British government that had neither the will nor the cash to embark on such endeavours.

"Our burden is too great," William Gladstone once complained to Rhodes. "We have too much… to do. Apart from increasing our obligations in every part of the world, what advantage do you see to the English race in the acquisition of new territory?" Rhodes replied sharply: "Great Britain is a small island. Its position depends on her trade, and if we do not open up the dependencies of the world which are at present devoted to barbarism, we shall shut out the world's trade. It must be brought home to you that your trade is the world, and your life is the world, not England."

"I contend that we are the first race in the world, and that the more of the world we inhabit the better it is for the human race… If there be a God, I think that what he would like me to do is paint as much of the map of Africa British Red as possible."

– *Cecil John Rhodes*

"We must find new lands from which we can easily obtain raw materials and at the same time exploit the cheap slave labour that is available from the natives of the colonies. The colonies would also provide a dumping ground for the surplus goods produced in our factories."

– *Cecil John Rhodes*

But Rhodes was not overly hindered by the lack of will from the motherland. He had both the cash and the ambition to pursue whatever grand plans he devised – and he wasn't limited by his imagination, once famously declaring, "I would annex the planets, if I could. I often think of that."

The road to the stars is a long one, and for Rhodes it led through Matabeleland in modern-day Zimbabwe. He made many visits to the area over the years, but initially failed to secure a mining concession from the Ndebele king Lobengula, son of Mzilikazi. *(See Shaka.)* On another attempt in 1888 he was more devious, and thus more successful. Lobengula was promised that no more than ten white men would mine in his territory, but the clause was left out of the document the king actually signed. Armed with this dodgy concession, Rhodes received a charter from the UK government allowing him to prospect and to raise concessions from the Zambezi River to the great lakes of central Africa. Rhodes's dream of a railway line running from the Cape to Cairo was getting ever closer and, with the business of empire subcontracted to his company, little was going to stand in the way of his ambitions. The one fly in the ointment, though, was his failure to bring what is now Botswana under his charter, and it left him furious. "It is humiliating to be utterly beaten by these niggers," he railed.

In effect Rhodes annexed more than a million square miles, simply taking it from its indigenous people. With his settlers invading their lands and occupying or establishing towns such Bulawayo and Salisbury (now Harare), the Ndebele and Shona inevitably ran out of patience and rebelled. They were eventually crushed in the two Matabele Wars, ending resistance to the British Empire's relentless march, under Rhodes's guidance, from the beaches of Muizenberg to the shores of Lake Tanganyika. En route millions of people were dispossessed and reduced to living as tenants in their own land.

> "So little done, so much to do."
> *– Cecil John Rhodes, overheard by his friend Lewis Michell on the day of his death*

Interestingly, by the time the Witwatersrand had been identified as the greatest gold reserve on Earth, in the early 1890s, Rhodes's financial savvy had seemingly deserted him. He made huge blunders speculating on gold, investing in miles of dead ground while missing the bargains that would make the Randlords some of the richest people in the world. He was clearly distracted. He had made his fortune and by then his ambition transcended material needs. His time for Empire building had come, and he spent the last decade of his life attempting to make the Cape Colony the most powerful "country" in Africa. He plotted, he schemed, he wrangled. When objections were raised, complainants were "squared" – his favoured euphemism for passing a bribe – and problems disappeared. Surrounded by yes men, his megalomania soared and, eventually, his judgment failed.

By the mid-1890s, there seemed but one genuine obstacle in Rhodes's way. The Transvaal Republic, with its newly discovered mineral wealth, remained stubbornly anti-British and protectionist under the leadership of Paul Kruger. In 1895, the same year that the vast territory falling under the BSAC north of the Limpopo was officially named Rhodesia (now Zambia and Zimbabwe), Rhodes agitated for and then supported a calamitous raid on the Transvaal that had planned to join forces with a rebellion of disenfranchised *uitlanders* – "foreign" residents in the republic, mostly British, who had flooded into the Boer republic since the gold rush of 1886. *(See Lord Milner.)*

But the *uitlanders* failed to rise up and the Jameson Raid ended in abject failure, causing great consternation and political retribution across the country and back in Britain. Rhodes was forced to resign as prime minister, and the affair ultimately proved to be a primary cause of the Anglo-Boer War four years later – as Jan Smuts phrased it in 1906, it "was the real declaration of war".

Rhodes died of heart failure in Muizenberg in 1902 three months before his fiftieth birthday. Tens of thousands of Capetonians came to pay their respects at his Groote Schuur estate and then outside parliament, from where his funeral service began. Thousands more South Africans turned out to see his funeral train pass through on its way to Bulawayo, from where it was taken into the Matopo Hills in Matabeleland where crowds of Ndebele gave him "a royal salute".

Cecil John Rhodes was in many senses a "great" man. His name and marks are left across southern Africa, noticeably in Cape Town, where his prominent memorial looks down over the university and the city beyond, and in Grahamstown where the university bears his name. He is usually remembered by South Africans for his eponymous scholarships, which send the brightest and best to Oxford University. And for more than eighty years he even had a country named after him. But his legacy is far darker than that, and is widely evident in the politics of southern Africa in the past fifty years, particularly in the actions of the leaders of apartheid South Africa and of Mbeki and Mugabe.

It was Rhodes who first redistributed land along racial lines, often with appalling violence. It was Rhodes who controlled the media and used paid mercenaries to put his opponents to the sword. It was Rhodes who encouraged a political culture of corruption and self-aggrandising power-mongering, surrounding himself with appeasers and sycophants and ignoring the wants and needs of the citizens of the land.

And it was Rhodes who introduced violent land grabs in the nation to our north a century before its current travails began. Indeed, it's hard to see where the PAC was wrong when it said that "the problems which were being blamed on Mugabe were created by British colonialism, whose agent Cecil Rhodes used armed force to acquire land for settlers". Mugabe's insanity aside, there can be little doubt that the lingering resentment that has fuelled his destruction of Zimbabwe was caused by Cecil John Rhodes's wholesale theft of a vast stretch of Africa, and his utter disregard for whose who had once owned it.

Rhodes not only maintained a shockingly racist view of Africa and Africans; he regrettably had the money and the political clout to go a long way to achieving his ambitions. The rest of Africa is perhaps fortunate that he died when he did.

Jackie Selebi

b. 7 March 1950

Former National Commissioner of the SAPS; former
president of Interpol; crime denier; friend of the mafia;
fraudster; national disgrace

THE STORY OF JACOB SELLO SELEBI, commonly known as Jackie, is another sad tale of a legacy ruined, a fallen hero. Here was a man who sacrificed a great deal to help free his country – he was arrested for his activism in 1970s, he went into exile, he ran the ANC Youth League, he became a member of the ANC's National Executive Committee – and who is now destined to spend a good decade or so in prison. Such a pity that, having helped liberate the nation, he felt the need to sell it down the river quite so spectacularly, and in quite such an internationally notable manner. How did it ever go so wrong?

After the ANC was unbanned, Selebi returned to South Africa in 1991 and was put in charge of repatriating exiled ANC members and other anti-apartheid activists. It is said that he and Thabo Mbeki were close.

Selebi was elected as an MP in 1994, but it wasn't long before the Mandela administration sent him off to New York to represent South Africa at the United Nations. That continued for three years and, after a session in the department of foreign affairs as director general, his old mate Thabo asked him to take on the role of police commissioner in 2000.

This was classic Mbeki. The president, you'll remember, didn't really rate South Africa's crime problem. He thought it was all a racist whinge, so he saw no problem in appointing an old exile chum who'd never worn a uniform in his life as chief of police. Selebi seemed to fit all the political requirements of the job – that is, he was loyal to Mbeki – and he pleased enough people to be elevated to the presidency of Interpol in 2004. He was now in an extremely powerful position and had the opportunity to make a difference to the lives of South Africans reeling from the wave of violent crime that had hit the country.

Instead, his time in charge was to be catastrophic. Apart from anything else, Selebi was just a crap policeman. Embarrassingly overweight, he hardly inspired confidence in his subordinates, the poor guys on the sharp end of South Africa's battle against crime. He wobbled about in his uniform like some kind of enormous jelly in a duvet cover, and he saw no harm in describing a young female officer as a chimpanzee.

Amusingly, he thought it perfectly reasonable to suggest that prostitution and the drug trade be legalised for the duration of the Soccer World Cup. This was really cunning. You see, if you legalise a whole load of nasty stuff then there won't be any actual crime to worry about while people go about pimping their daughters and selling mandrax to 12-year-olds. Naturally, civil society was appalled, and the top cop's brilliant scheme was quietly shelved. The notion that we should turn South Africa into a vast whorehouse and crack den – but only, of course, while the whole world was watching – was so mad as to be laughable.

> "Jackie Selebi drives around in a stolen car, is quite open about his friendship with a known mafioso and brazenly sports a moustache looted off Charles Bronson's face."
>
> *– Andrew Donaldson*

Less amusing was his attitude to his job. "What's all the fuss about crime?" he nonchalantly remarked in 2007, infuriating the millions of South Africans concerned with our fifty-a-day murder rate. When taken to task on the comment, he expanded: "We do have crime in South Africa. Nobody has denied it. But to exaggerate the point and speak about a crisis… A crisis means total disorder. I'm sure what we experience, everyone around the world experiences." He truly was Mbeki's man.

Beyond the incompetence and negligence, however, there were the actual dirty deeds.

As it all came out in the court case, Selebi had a friend. A friend called Glenn Agliotti. Now, as Selebi was himself told in 2002, Agliotti was a drug smuggler and a gangster. But he was a rich one, and Selebi liked sharp suits and a bit of retail therapy for him and his wife every now and then. So his friend offered to help him out with a few thousand rand here and a Louis Vuitton handbag there. Then it became R120,000 here and R200,000 there. In the end, these bribes were to amount to more than R1.2 million. Rather like the Zuma-Shaik relationship, Agliotti had the chief of police on retainer. *(See Schabir Shaik.)*

Bribes being bribes, there had to be something in return, so Selebi kept an eye out for his mate, using his position at Interpol, among other things, show Agliotti a document indicating that MI5 and MI6 were tracking him.

When eventually questioned on this hugely unsuitable relationship with a convicted drug smuggler – the police chief hanging out with the mafia don – Selebi was insulted: they were just friends and they never discussed crime, he declared, "finished and klaar".

Mbeki, being Mbeki, did nothing. Loyalty, remember. In fact, he implored a meeting of religious leaders to trust him on Selebi the week after Agliotti was arrested for the murder of Brett Kebble in November 2006.

But eventually it all became a bit too obvious and a bit too much. In September of the following year, the National Prosecuting Authority had Selebi arrested on charges of corruption, racketeering, fraud and defeating the ends of justice. He was given an extended leave of absence (on full pay) – with the result that South Africa didn't have a national police commissioner for a year and a half – while the court case went ahead, and he quit his position at Interpol. Despite the jaunty arrogance that would characterise his behaviour in court over the next couple of years, the Selebi ship was going down. He was convicted of corruption in July 2010.

One can't do much better than quote Judge Meyer Joffe during the sentencing: "You were aware of the high honour that was bestowed on you. You must have been an embarrassment to all right-thinking citizens of this country. I am satisfied that a sentence of 15 years is an appropriate sentence."

But the judge wasn't done, going on to condemn the manner in which the country's most senior policeman had conducted himself in court. Selebi's evidence was "mendacious and in some cases manufactured", Joffe said. "It is inconceivable that the person who occupied the office of the national commissioner of police could have been such a stranger to the truth. At no stage during the trial did the accused display any remorse."

It was damning stuff. And all the while the crime outside continued. Great savage waves of it.

"What's all the fuss about crime?" Indeed. So sorry to have bothered you.

Schabir Shaik

b 10 December 1956

Businessman; friend and financial adviser to Jacob
Zuma; convicted fraudster; parole violator; medical
miracle; icon of modern South African corruption

PERHAPS IT IS THE BEWILDERING LEVELS of poverty in South Africa that drives it. Alternatively, perhaps it is something strangely South African that sees ordinary men driven to invest their sense of self in the things they own, as opposed to what they have achieved. It's not good enough to have just a house and a car, because a big and important man has a great many cars and several houses. If his religion or culture allows for it, he might have many wives too.

Jacob Zuma is famously such a big man. Yet, as famously, he never really had the means to support the life of a big man. This problematic chasm between the way Zuma saw himself, in 1990, and the actual fact of his financial situation, was spotted by the brothers Shaik, of Durban. Schabir Shaik, in particular, known as the more flamboyant of the bunch, would go on to cultivate Zuma's pomposity and self-importance over the years by assisting him when and where necessary. And, as various South African courts would find, he didn't do it for free.

In all cases with Zuma's shenanigans you have to bear in mind his history: how he was born poor, how he was never formally educated, how he was in the care of the ANC all his adult life. When he returned from exile and was given a government job in 1994 – he became MEC for tourism and economic affairs in KwaZulu-Natal – he was expected to just get on with it. He wouldn't have known how to.

But Schabir Shaik can make no claims to such naivety. He saw Zuma coming, and – with great foresight, we must admit – predicted that Zuma would one day go far. And so the interest-free loans started to flow. All in, they were eventually calculated to have exceeded R1.2 million in value. Shaik established himself as Zuma's "financial advisor", so he would have seen the figures, and he would have known that, on the salary of an MEC, there was no way in hell Zuma could ever repay him. In cash terms, that is.

Indeed, when the law finally caught up with Shaik, his conviction for fraud – as opposed to the corruption conviction – was related to the sudden and irregular writing off in 1999 of more than a million rands' worth of "loans" made out to Zuma. As advocated for the state Billy Downer would describe it, Shaik had put Zuma on retainer. (Downer also ruthlessly exposed Shaik as a charlatan and liar – *see box*.)

Downer: Mr Shaik, you have admitted all your qualifications as stated on letterheads and brochures are false.
Shaik: Yes.
Downer: It says here you have an MBA.
Shaik: I don't have an MBA.
Downer: I have an Nkobi brochure here. Your CV is noted. It says "graduate of prestigious universities in Europe and the United States".
Shaik: I am not.
Downer: It says you are a qualified engineer.
Shaik: I am not.
Downer: It says you are a business creator.
Shaik: Thank you.
Downer: It says you are a published author.
Shaik: It is also incorrect.
Downer: How did this happen?
Shaik: I don't want to explain how one develops a sense of confidence. I used it to promote confidence and impress clients.
Downer: Your CV also mentions your link to Jacob Zuma.
Shaik: Yes.
Downer: To impress customers?
Shaik: No. Where one deals with foreign customers they need to understand the political stability in SA. It was a way to help them understand.
– Transcript of cross-examination of Schabir Shaik
by prosecutor Billy Downer, Durban High Court, February 2005

Having bought his man, Shaik, under the guise of his company Nkobi Holdings, then formed a relationship with the French arms company Thomson CSF. Together they created a South African company, Thomson Holdings, and after a couple of trial runs at tendering for contracts, such as that for making the new South African driver's licence, Shaik decided it was time to go after some real money. The pot of gold was an obvious one: the new, very large arms acquisition.

This time, there were billions and billions of rands up for grabs, and Shaik wanted a piece of the pie. Fortunately for him, his brother, Chippy, worked in the defence department's acquisitions division. Plus, he had Zuma. All of a sudden, it looked like his long-term investment might pay off.

As 1999 progressed, Zuma, ever focused on the grave matters of state, was also busy building a large traditional Zulu-style residential village near Nkandla in KwaZulu-Natal. Unsurprisingly, he didn't have the money for it so, in order to get it built, Shaik solicited on Zuma's behalf a bribe of R1 million from Thomson Holdings. In return, Zuma was supposed to protect the company from any investigations into the arms deal, and also ensure a continued flow of government contracts. It is for this influence that Shaik was willing to corrupt the country. South Africa's nascent democracy was of no real interest to him. It was all about making money. Not good money, not money on which you might live well, but obscene amounts of money.

While Zuma's charges were dropped on a technicality, Shaik was jailed for his crimes in 2006. In convicting him to fifteen years behind bars, Judge Hilary Squires described him as "a man untroubled by a resort to duplicity or falsehood to gain one's end", living "as if he existed in a bubble of his own preoccupation and belief system". He stopped short of calling him a scumbag, but it wasn't hard to read between the lines.

Shaik, however, wasn't done with his assault on the South African justice system just yet. Having served little more than two years of his sentence, much of it in hospital rather than prison, he was mysteriously granted medical parole, a concession supposedly reserved for terminally ill prisoners in their last dying months. At the time there was a public outcry; no vaguely savvy South African believed for a second that he was at death's door, or that the deal was above board. That it happened a mere month before Jacob Zuma assumed the presidency, and that Shaik remains alive nearly two years on from his release – merrily violating parole when the mood takes him – leaves that collective opinion unchanged.

Having corrupted the highest officials in the land for his personal gain, Shaik has gone on to make a mockery of justice in South Africa. Indeed, his effrontery seems to know no bounds. In an interview with the *Rapport*, after the newspaper exposed him breaking his parole, he was questioned about rumours of an impending presidential pardon. "Why should I even be asking for a pardon?" he demanded testily. "If three people were part of a so-called plot to elicit funds from the French, why are the French free, why is the president free and why is Shaik still sitting as a convict?"

The obvious retort would have been to suggest to the affronted Mr Shaik that he had posed a very good question – it's just that he was asking it back to front.

But Shaik has been at the vanguard of making the new South Africa a place where greased palms and shady deals are just par for the course; where no government tender is awarded without the rank stench of fraud and corruption filling the air; where if two people are accused of a crime and only one is convicted then the logic of the day determines that he is in fact innocent.

Schabir Shaik has made us a laughing stock and has done inestimable damage to the country as a whole. Every leader of every important country on Earth knows all about our president and the tightrope he has walked to avoid jail time. Shaik was his voice of temptation, his Mephistopheles, and it will come as no surprise if his pardon eventually comes from the highest office in the land. Then, just like the devil, he will once again be free to spread his poisonous ways.

Shaka

c. 1787 – 22 September 1828

King of the Zulus (1816-1828); instigator of the Mfecane; mastermind behind the expansion of the Zulu empire; subjugator and unifier of peoples; military visionary; brutal and murderous tyrant

HISTORY HAS IT THAT WITH KING SHAKA you trod carefully, for he was a man who would order your execution without so much as a second thought. To some extent you still need to tread carefully around the Zulu king. There is a powerful post-colonial revisionist lobby that asks serious questions of the received knowledge about the brutal and bloodthirsty King Shaka of the Zulus, the military genius and conqueror of African tribes. They point out, not without reason, that the picture of the noble savage held great sway among racists and romantics alike, and that there is very little cast-iron evidence to place Shaka at the scene of the crime.

The problem, of course, is that we just don't know, and this insistence on documentation, on cast-iron proof, is in its own way Eurocentric. The people living in modern-day KwaZulu-Natal in the late 1700s and early 1800s didn't write their stories; they told them. Zulu history has a huge oral tradition, demonstrated in the beautiful, lyrical and lilting Hlonipha poetry and praise songs, and the many examples in praise of Shaka establish that, revisionism or not, King Shaka was the *man* in early 1800s Zululand.

The story of Shaka is hotly contested and mixed up with matters of race, history and, naturally, pride. These days the man has an international airport named after him, as well as a stage musical. In post-apartheid South Africa, it seems the way we're going is lionisation.

This may be politically correct, but the argument that imperialism and the slaughter of innocent civilians is wrong whether you're black or white is more than reasonable. And Shaka was the driving force behind a period in South African history known as the Mfecane – variously translated along the lines of "upheaval" or "annihilation" – a violent ripple effect that would spread from the beautiful rolling hills of Zululand, near modern-day Melmoth, where he was born, to deep into today's Zimbabwe, Mozambique, Malawi, Botswana, Lesotho and Swaziland

KING
SHAKA
1787-1828

There is even a place in the Caprivi Strip with a Zulu name – Katima Mulilo – "the place where the fire was put out".

Shaka, so far as we know, was born out of wedlock sometime in the 1780s when his father Senzangakhona, a young chief of a small and irrelevant clan, the Zulu, met a woman called Nandi of the Langeni. But Senzangakhona denied impregnating Nandi, saying her lack of menstruation must have been due to *ushaka*, an intestinal bug.

The story goes that Nandi and her son were bullied and harassed, and that they eventually settled under the wing of Dingiswayo of the Mthethwa, to whom the Zulus were subservient. He soon joined an *ibutho*, or regiment, and served as a warrior under Dingiswayo, some say with distinction.

Upon the death of Senzangakhona, Shaka returned to claim the Zulu chieftainship with the help of Dingiswayo. It was 1816, and Shaka took much of what he had learnt from Dingiswayo and adopted it for his new chiefdom, famously instituting the *amabutho* system of age-based regiments, dismissing the throwing assegai as a weapon of preference and developing the short-handled *iklwa* stabbing spear instead. He also introduced the now-famous "horns of the buffalo" battle formation. In a flash, the Zulus were militarised.

It was an interesting time in the region. Portuguese slave traders were operating out of what is now Maputo, there was white encroachment into the interior and the trekkers were soon to start moving north. At the time the Zulus were one of many clans in the region, including the Mthethwa, the Dlamini and the Qwabe.

When Zwide, chief of the Ndwandwe, had Shaka's old mentor Dingiswayo murdered, the leaderless Mthethwa turned to Shaka for assistance. The end result was the 1818 battle of Gqokli Hill, where Shaka's army was victorious despite being outnumbered two to one. As many as 7,000 Ndwandwe were killed.

Shaka's martial leadership in the Ndwandwe-Zulu War against Zwide makes for fascinating reading, and let there be no doubt that the man was indeed a military genius. There was, however, a downside to his extended campaign of violence: the depredations of his impis were starting to have a serious impact outside of what we now know as Zululand. Such was the all-out savagery of his armies that those who had angered Shaka, or somehow survived the Zulu onslaught, felt compelled to leave the area, and many of these displaced peoples in turn used Zulu tactics to clear their paths.

The war with the Ndwandwe can be seen as the epicentre of the Mfecane. Under Shaka, the Zulus only assimilated women and children into the nation; men of fighting age and the elderly were simply killed. And Shaka's army was schooled in brutality. The punishment for any sign of weakness was death by clubbing, so mercy was not high on the warrior's agenda.

The great Ndwandwe general Soshangane survived the war with Shaka and invaded an area in Mozambique, where he subjugated a number of peoples using Shaka's techniques. He then assisted slave traders, making them pay tribute. Another Ndwandwe general, Zwangendaba, accompanied Soshangane for a time, but then kept on moving north, again using Shaka's tactics to forge his way. His people, the Ngoni, eventually settled in an area now split between Zambia, Malawi and Tanzania. Mzilikazi of the Khumalo clan, one of Shaka's generals, established a nation known as the Ndebele, or Matabele, in what is now Bulawayo in southern Zimbabwe, violently displacing the Shona along the way, who moved north towards the Zambezi. Accounts vary, but they say Mzilikazi's forces left a trail of corpses and destruction wherever they went.

> He is Shaka the unshakeable,
> Thunderer-while-sitting, son of Menzi.
> He is the bird that preys on other birds,
> The battle-axe that excels over other battle-axes in sharpness,
> He is the long-strided pursuer, son of Ndaba,
> Who pursued the sun and the moon.
> He is the great hubbub like the rocks of Nkandla
> Where elephants take shelter
> When the heavens frown
>
> *– Translation of traditional praise song celebrating Shaka*

These are just a sample of the effects of the Mfecane. Taken together, it was a staggering time of upheaval, and – though recent interpreters of history prefer to assign blame, to varying degrees, beyond just the Zulus – most of it boiled down to the brutality of one man: Shaka.

An indication of how the revered chief was quite probably psychopathic was his reaction to the death of his mother, Nandi, in 1827. In order that his people would feel and understand his pain, Shaka ordered that all pregnant women and their husbands be executed and in a horrific massacre some 7,000 of Shaka's people were put to the spear.

Shaka's mental state veered beyond just brutal irrationality into the realms of sheer paranoia, too. He rejected the idea of ever having children, fearing an heir would try to kill him, so if ever a concubine or lover fell pregnant he would have her killed. Ultimately, though, his paranoia proved to be a self-fulfilling prophecy.

Not long after the Nandi massacre, Shaka's half-brothers Dingane and Mhlangana assassinated him with the help of an aide. *(See Dingane.)*

By the time of his death, Shaka had expanded the Zulu empire so that he ruled over some 250,000 people and could muster a huge army of crack troops. His impact had been felt, and would continue to be felt, far beyond the borders of Zululand and deep into southern Africa. It is impossible to say how many people died on Shaka's direct orders, but the number is at least in the tens of thousands, ranking him as one of, if not the, greatest individual tyrant in South African history. So next time you fly into King Shaka International, it's worth wondering what exactly there is to celebrate about the first king of the mighty Zulu empire.

Stella Sigcau

4 January 1937 – 7 May 2006

Pondo princess; first female Prime Minister of Transkei;
Minister of Public Enterprises (1994-1999) and Public
Works (1999-2006); prime example of ruling-party
protectionism in the face of deleterious incompetence

IT'S NOT BECAUSE OF THE BRIBERY that Stella Sigcau takes her place here, sandwiched as she is between Shaka and Rudolf Straeuli. Yes, she had "an established record of venality", as one writer so handsomely phrased it, but you just need to flip back a few pages to the "dying" fraudster on parole if you want a proper example of the destructive corruption that besets our leadership. By contrast, Sigcau's dabbling with the receipts was small fry. Nothing, really. Kind of like her contribution to the governance of this country in the 12 years she spent in parliament. Which was the real problem.

But back to the bribery, just for a moment. Sigcau, a Pondo princess, actually started out her political career in the notoriously dirty Transkei government as a driving force for anti-corruption, taking over in 1987 as prime minister when George Matanzima was muscled out. There was, as a result, much fury when her participation in a dodgy deal with Matanzima and Sol Kerzner emerged not long after she assumed office. *(See Sol Kerzner.)* Bantu Holomisa, who helped expose much of the corruption, ousted her in a coup, and she later admitted to the Alexander Commission that she had benefited to the tune of R50,000 after Kerzner's illicit payment to Matanzima. Here was her explanation: "Knowing African tradition as I do, how could I as a leader of the Pondos reject a gift from the Tembu royalty without offending the giver?" Though she lost her premiership of the Transkei, she was never charged.

And with that, to the point. Because if "African tradition" allows the acceptance of bribes, then it seems that a similar kind of political tradition has emerged in our current government allowing for the acceptance of inertia and incompetence in leadership roles. And this can be far more damaging in the greater scheme of things than the occasional kickback falling from the sky.

In Sigcau's case, there is widespread consensus that she failed in both her ministries. In less diplomatic terms, she was transcendentally useless. Her *Sunday Times* obituary said of her, "as a minister in three post-apartheid governments she seemed to be so inactive that it was easy to forget her existence. When she was remembered it was only to ask why she was still in the government... Her entire period of high office was characterised by inactivity." And her DA "report cards" were as damning; for example, only Manto Tshabalala-Msimang received worse ratings – and that's because she was actively bad, whereas Sigcau – well, she just did nothing.

"If you give a job to Stella Sigcau, nothing happens."
– *Quote appearing in the Financial Mail in 1998, paralleled in her Sunday Times obituary in 2006, and seemingly widely echoed by government insiders and her own staff*

As Minister of Public Enterprises for five years, she had state assets worth about R50 billion at her disposal, yet she couldn't work out what do with them. She ensured, for example, that Eskom had no plan whatsoever for future energy creation. *(See Alec Erwin.)* As Minister of Public Works after that, she was arguably worse. She came in for particular criticism in 2004 – from political commentators, opposition parties and even ANC MPs – for her ministry's near-complete failure to meet deadlines on the government's important and much-anticipated Expanded Public Works Programme, which was supposed to be an important step in the battle to fight unemployment. Allegations of "corruption, bribery, unauthorised spending and failure to follow tender procedures" also haunted her tenure.

And yet, despite even the telling complaints from within her party, the powers that be simply threw up their kneejerk defences and took no action. As historian RW Johnson later wrote, the "fact that the ANC was far more concerned to protect Sigcau from criticism than it was with her neglect of the Programme showed how unserious the government really was about dealing with unemployment". In other words, they were unserious about making a better life for pretty much half the country's population (and ironically the ANC's voting base).

Time and again Sigcau was defended by her political comrades, right up to the highest level, in parliament and to the press, and time and again she got off. When she died of heart failure in 2006, her party comrades could not point to one lasting achievement of hers – after *12 years* in the cabinet.

The reason she never got the boot, it goes almost without saying, was pure politics. Due to her royal heritage, she was a guaranteed vote-bagger in the Transkei – and what more can you ask from a minister, seems to be the ANC's attitude. It truly is a disastrous way to go about the running of a country – especially when election victories don't really hang in the balance here – and it is indicative of the ruling party's desire to remain entrenched at the top come what may and the poor be damned.

Sigcau is by no means a stand-alone example of stagnant inadequacy within the ANC leadership in the past decade and a half. Far from it. Ministers such as Nosiviwe Mapisa-Nqakula, Membathisi Mdladlana, Brigitte Mabandla and the profoundly hopeless Ivy Matsepe-Casaburri can all lay claim to the top spot. But Sigcau is their champion. And, as such, she will have to wear the mantle for them and all the others who have stepped into cabinet and then sat about on their underperforming bottoms wondering what to do with themselves.

Rudolf Straeuli

b. 20 August 1963

Springbok rugby player (1994-1995); Springbok coach
(2002-2003); Springbok embarrassment (2002-2003)

THE WORST THING ABOUT IT was that it was so obviously the plan. This wasn't a heat-of-the-moment, reflexive instance of violence. It was the strategy. In a moment that still shames the colours green and gold, Jannes Labuschagne shoulder-charged Jonny Wilkinson hard and at full pelt after he had made a clearance kick. The tackle was so late that the ball had practically landed when the giant lock smashed into the English fly half's midriff. Luckily, Wilkinson wasn't hospitalised, but he was replaced later in the game after yet another illegal hit, and was ruled out of rugby for a month.

It was November 2002, and the Springbok brains trust, for want of a better term, had evidently decided they would risk players being sent off the field – Labuschagne was, to no-one's surprise, red-carded – in exchange for ending Wilkinson's game early. It was a tactic typical of an era of Springbok rugby for which all right-thinking South Africans feel nothing but shame. The Boks' savagery that day at Twickenham – the head-butting, the elbowing, the gouging, the stamping, the punching – won't easily be forgotten by anyone who saw it. Labuschagne's offence wasn't even the worst on show; that dubious distinction went to captain on the day Corné Krige, who spent the game pretending he was in a cage-fighting tournament rather than playing rugby.

This, then, was the era of Rudolf Straeuli.

Speaking to sane, rugby-loving South Africans about this time in Bok rugby is remarkable. Bok fans are the most passionate in the game, often blindly so, but most will agree that it took them some years to forgive the green and gold for what happened during Straeuli's time at the helm. By the end, it was so bad that many hoped for Springbok losses just so Straeuli might be shown the door sooner.

Internationally, the Twickenham debacle cemented a general feeling that the Boks were little more than a bunch of borderline psychopathic goons existing on the edge of criminality. It's a reputation that dies hard. If Bok fans ever wonder why referees can seem especially watchful when South Africa are on the field, send an email of thanks to Mr Straeuli. The Springboks have never backed down on the rugby field, but the "brutal Boks" were his creation.

The Springboks, despite their shockingly violent play at Twickenham that day, went on to lose 53-3, their worst defeat ever and doubtless the most shameful day in Bok history. Never in the history of the sport was such a thumping more deserved. At the post-match press conference, the boneheaded Straeuli reacted like a scolded child, instantly on the defensive. "We have two players concussed. Do you think we concussed ourselves?" he sneered. Laughably, TV footage would reveal exactly that: Krige himself throwing a vicious punch during a maul, missing the intended English victim, Matt Dawson, and landing square on André Pretorius's face instead.

"On the first night, the winners of the tug-of-war had been promised food. Our group won and they brought a box which contained two live chickens. 'There's your supper, there's the fire, do whatever you want,' said Rudolf. The Afrikaans guys said: 'Lekker, we can sort this out and share the meat.' But Rudolf said: 'No, no, no! Joe [van Niekerk], you must kill the first chicken.'

Now, Joe was the type of guy who thought chickens came from Nando's. He had never considered how they got there, so he started to panic and hyperventilate. 'No, I can't kill a chicken!' he said.

'Joe, kill the chicken, just wring its fucking neck,' Rudolf replied. 'It's easy.'

Joe had never killed anything in his life, and wrenched the poor creature's neck, without too much conviction. I can't explain how horrific it was. We all stood there like bloody barbarians watching poor Joe hyperventilate and reluctantly torture the unfortunate fowl. He just didn't want to do it and didn't know how. Eventually Joost van der Westhuizen had to intervene by grabbing the chicken and putting it out of its misery."

– *Extract from Captain In The Cauldron by John Smit*

Magnanimity is a long word – too long for Straeuli – who bitterly refused to apologise and sent a supposed warning shot to Clive Woodward's England. "We'll see you in Perth," he muttered, in reference to the next England/South Africa fixture in the opening rounds of the 2003 World Cup.

Despite his faux swagger, Straeuli's team deservedly saw their arses in that match, too, and subsequently lost to New Zealand in the quarterfinals. The Springboks, now renowned as cheats, poor losers and brawlers, were sent home, and the rugby world was pleased. From London to Dunedin, Sydney to Paris, the

Boks were roundly despised.

Straeuli had repeatedly told the media that he ought to be judged on the 2003 World Cup, and that anything leading up to it was part of the process of building a Springbok team that would win the tournament. He had started off well enough when he took over from Harry Viljoen in 2002, with victories over Wales, Argentina and Samoa, but as soon as the Boks came up against top international opposition their coach's lack of nous was quickly found out. The Straeuli brand of rugby – which can be roughly summarised as *domkrag* rugby or, if you will, *donner 'n moer* – was hauled out week after week, and South African rugby fans watched with horror as the green and gold was dragged through the foulest mud by a succession of humiliating defeats and a sporting reputation in free fall. A single (narrow) victory in the ensuing Tri-Nations was followed by record defeats against France at Stade Vélodrome (30-10), Scotland at Murrayfield (21-6), England at Twickenham (53-3) and, the following year, against New Zealand at Loftus Versfeld (52-16). For good measure, and to heap shame upon humiliation, there was even a race row, when Geo Cronje refused to share a room with his coloured team-mate, Quinton Davids, at a training camp.

By the time the World Cup eventually kicked off, Straeuli's coaching record against major opposition was played 10, lost 8. By the end of the competition, it was played 12, lost 10.

Amazingly, he didn't resign straight away. He had an appalling record, he had utterly demolished the Bok brand and he was widely loathed by fans and players alike – and yet he still didn't get the hint. It took the revelation of his greatest embarrassment yet for the clamour from rugby-loving South Africans to penetrate his impressive kop. In the end, it was Kamp Staaldraad that sunk him.

The story of Kamp Staaldraad remains utterly mind-boggling. Even after years of reflection it seems unbelievable that, in this day and age, the events of those few days actually took place. After picking his squad for Australia, Straeuli ordered them to a police training base near Thabazimbi, whereupon they were subjected to an astonishing series of boot camp-type assaults designed, apparently, to remove the players' sense of self and create a single, unified team.

Building team spirit is one thing, but this was insane. Rugby is a game that thrives on dazzling moments of individual genius. A Joost van der Westhuizen dummy-and-run, an André Pretorius drop goal, Breyton Paulse dancing around a tackle. By removing this from the game, you take away the beauty of rugby and turn it into grinding gridiron. A well-organised team creates space for the individual. The idea of creating a squad of hyper-violent automatons, apart from anything else, was just bad rugby.

But Straeuli, in his wisdom, figured it was just what the team needed. Over the next few days, his ex-police buddies forced the players to strip and leopard-crawl, naked, over gravel. They were coerced into a freezing-cold lake, naked, where they spent hours trying to pump up rugby balls. When Krige and other players eventually tried to get out of the water, instructors fired shots past them to force them back in. Later, the players were herded, naked, into a muddy pits, where icy water was pumped onto them as *God Save The Queen* and the haka were played at ear-splitting volume, time after time, hour after hour. Further trials followed: one-on-one fist fights, two days of sleep deprivation, hours spent carrying around rocks and poles, an ugly incident involving a chicken having its neck wrung.

It was brutal and ridiculous, and yet it expressed so eloquently the ugliness of Straeuli's intent. That it was England and New Zealand that booted the Boks out of the 2003 World Cup was, in its own way, poetic. And entirely predictable.

When pictures of Staaldraad found their way into national newspapers, it proved to be the belated end of Straeuli's career. The rugby world in general, and Springbok fans in particular, were shocked by the images of the cream of South African rugby – national heroes – naked, wretched, filthy, freezing, exhausted and humiliated. At last, Straeuli was shown the door. But not before receiving one of the least-deserved golden handshakes in history, reportedly around R2 million.

Sadly, Straeuli's demise was not the end of the story because tragedy then followed farce. The Staaldraad whistle-blower turned out to be Bok video analyst Dale McDermott, who was subsequently made a scapegoat in SA rugby circles for breaking ranks about the camp, even though persistent rumours had made revelations inevitable. He lost his job and was shamefully ostracised as a Judas. When Jake White attempted to hire him back, SA Rugby vetoed the appointment. He was forced out of rugby entirely, and in the course of the following year he sank into depression. He shot himself in January 2005.

Sanity returned to the Springboks under White and his captain John Smit. These two men are South Africans we can be proud of; men who embody that ability to rise from the ashes. Smit has become a titan of the game in the intervening years: smart, well-spoken and hugely respected around the world. Tellingly, in the context of the era that he survived, he is considered one of the hardest men in the sport, and the Springboks remain one of the physically toughest teams in the world. It's just that White and Smit managed to meld that toughness with an actual playing strategy, and their World Cup victory in 2007 marked the moment of rehabilitation of South African rugby for many fans across the world. They had won, deservingly, by playing good hard rugby to a well-conceived game plan.

Amazing, isn't it, that it took four years to wash the stench of Rudolf Straeuli from the green and gold shirt? His reign typified ugly, stupid rugby, and will forever be a blot on our proud sporting history.

Mike Sutcliffe

b. 1 October 1954

Municipal Manager, eThekwini, Durban; consummate
ANC apparatchik; racially and politically polarising
name-changer extraordinaire

MANY RESIDENTS OF JOHANNESBURG LOOK AT DURBAN with longing in their eyes – and with good reason. Johannesburg is a shockingly badly run city, and when you call the infamous "Joburg Connect" number to report those all-too-common power cuts, water cuts, sewage leaks and broken roads, you're usually rewarded with the sound of a telephone ringing into infinity.

So, not only does Durban have beaches, a year-round summer and a successful rugby team, it also has eThekwini Municipality, which is undoubtedly the best ANC-run city council in South Africa. It is, as they go, fairly jacked up, and it is led by a much-unloved individual called Mike Sutcliffe, who features here not for incompetence or for being a racist or even for comparing the international Blue Flag beach-rating scheme to apartheid when several Durban beaches had their status revoked for being polluted, but for being the driving force behind something petty and vindictive, designed for no other reason than to hurt and offend.

Street renaming in this country is unnecessarily soaked in controversy. People who have a problem if DF Malan Drive is renamed Beyers Naude Drive or Hans Strijdom Drive becomes Malibongwe Drive just need to shut their dumb cakeholes. But the process needs to be motivated by the right reasons – to represent the people who live in the area and to offer a wider description of who created this country. That – and it really is fine – includes ANC figures.

Just up the road from Durban is the KwaZulu-Natal capital, Pietermaritzburg. Ironically, the town is one of the worst-run in South Africa, and a once-pretty Victorian settlement is now a waste-strewn dump that ought to shame those who run it. But they got the street-renaming thing right. By accepting the city's history, they decided to rename streets not named after people to honour those who had been left out. Hence, Pietermaritzburg still sports a Victoria Road and a Retief Street, but the former Longmarket Street is now named for Chief Langalibalele and Durban Road has become Alan Paton Drive. Seems fair enough.

But down the highway in Durban they were motivated by an obvious and rather ugly triumphalism. When it came to renaming streets, they decided, in a few cases, to outright offend – as in the renaming of Kingsway Road in Amanzimtoti to Andrew Zondo Road. As in Andrew Zondo, the young MK activist who planted a bomb at a shopping centre in Amanzimtoti in December 1985, which killed three women and two children, and injured forty.

> "At a recent KwaZulu-Natal Philharmonic Orchestra performance, he [Sutcliffe] was booed loudly on being introduced by director Bongani Tembe.
>   'I said to myself, is that what makes them happy? (It must be) some kind of white-male penis thing.'"
> – *Extract from "Durban's most hated man", Times Live, October 2009*

Zondo's story is complex and, hanged at age 19, he was undoubtedly a struggle martyr. Nonetheless, the murder of children is never justifiable and, more to the point, not cause for celebration. Attaching Zondo's name to a street that is used on a daily basis by friends and family of the people he killed is grossly insensitive. A cruel decision that flies in the face of reconciliation and nation-building, it implies to local ratepayers that its council applauds the deaths of those children.

While Zondo Road is perhaps the most objectionable of Sutcliffe's efforts, the decision to rename the Mangosuthu Buthelezi Highway after the ANC human-rights lawyer Griffiths Mxenge is just spiteful. And it coincided with the call to rename the Princess Magogo Stadium in KwaMashu in honour of Dumisane Makhaye. Magogo was Buthelezi's mother, which would lead the casual observer to believe that Sutcliffe is a vindictive stirrer who enjoys flaunting his power in the face of a waning IFP. Indeed, the behind-the-scenes theory goes that the provocative Durban name-changing spree may well have been a strategy to boost KwaZulu-Natal's declining ANC branch membership ahead of the 2009 elections by inflaming tensions between the ANC, IFP and DP. A theory only, and a deeply cynical one at that – but how else to explain some of the decisions made?

Much can be argued about the expensive renaming of apolitical landmarks, such as Ridge Street or Commercial Road, or even of the general choice of street names in Durban, and how the place is now reminiscent of that ruined city to the north, Maputo, with its Che Guevara, Swapo and Problem Mkhize roads. But that's just one side of the issue. It is the nasty, ugly use of deliberately upsetting names that exposes Sutcliffe for what he is – a really rather unpleasant fellow – and promotes political and racial polarisation in our communities.

Eugène Terre'Blanche

31 January 1941 – 3 April 2010

Founder of the AWB (1973-2010); leader of the "white right"; civil-war fomenter; white supremacist; criminal; national embarrassment

FOR THOSE WHO NEVER SUFFERED INSULT, offence or worse at their hands, the remaining few politically active white supremacists in this country eventually became figures of fun and derision. Oh, how amusing it was when Eugène Terre'Blanche fell off his horse; how funny to discover his underpants had holes in them.

It goes without saying that Terre'Blanche was funny to the liberal elite who looked down on him from afar. After all, ET (as he came to be known) was a living caricature and a societal troglodyte; a blithering backwards Boer with a stupid beard and an Anglophobia steeped in a history that was more than 110 years old. He revered the Boer War leaders such as Paul Kruger and generals De la Rey and De Wet. He spouted forth about apartheid and the superiority of the white race, even as the dark tone of his skin suggested an intimate mingling with the people he looked down on at some point in his familial past. He harked back endlessly to the Elysian pre-British days of the Christian Boerevolk, with their farms, their cattle and their idyllic pastoral existence. Before his death, he was writing his autobiography; it was to be called *Blouberge van Nimmer*. The blue mountains of long ago? What a twit, they giggled.

But, equally, it goes without saying that there was not much funny about Eugène Terre'Blanche to ordinary black people. As head of the AWB – the Afrikaner Resistance Movement, as its full title translates – he gave voice to a political philosophy that reduced the average South African to a "kaffir", to Verwoerd's hewer of wood. *(See HF Verwoerd.)* But it went further, dipping into the Nazi realm of race "science", of attempting to justify the subjugation of black people by stripping them of their humanity. "We do not hate blacks," Terre'Blanche once declared, in his deep voice that was to hypnotise an army of Calvinist right-wing supporters. "We just want to tell them to keep off our land."

So yes, the man was laughable to some, but the narrow-minded malice and

prejudice he brought to the political landscape of South Africa wrought far more damage than the mirth might suggest, and it nearly brought with it civil war.

Terre'Blanche established the AWB in 1973 in horror at the "liberal" policies of BJ Vorster, the prime minister at the time. Vorster, for the record, was imprisoned during the Second World War because of his pro-Nazi agitations. He had idolised his mentor and predecessor HF Verwoerd, but had ever so slightly relaxed certain apartheid policies in order to ease political pressure from within and outside the country. *(See BJ Vorster.)* For Terre'Blanche, this was unconscionable. He believed deeply in the Nationalist myth of the Boer victory at Blood River; that God had presented the land to His volk as He had offered Canaan to the Israelites. *(See Andries Pretorius.)* Vorster's approach would not do; hence Terre'Blanche's formation of a new party which, with its neo-Nazi swastika-type logo, left no-one in doubt as to its sentiments and ideals. The AWB would go on to oppose vehemently even the most pitiful offerings of restricted suffrage, such as those offered to Coloureds and Indians after the 1987 election.

Terre'Blanche and his organisation found prominence in 1979, when he and his supporters were convicted and fined for the tarring and feathering of one Professor Floors van Jaarsveld, who had dared to offer the opinion that the Day of the Vow was a public holiday without religious significance. As the 1980s drew on, he made it perfectly clear that he would deliberately tip South Africa into war if the National Party ever cleared the way for a Mandela presidency. A discovery of a huge arms cache on his brother's farm in 1982 proved as much. Terre'Blanche received a suspended sentence.

The AWB remained prominent throughout the decade and into the early 1990s when, with Mandela released and democracy looming, its agitations worsened. Believing the National Party, under FW de Klerk, was in the process of signing away his country and heritage, Terre'Blanche again predicted full-scale civil war. The government took his threats deadly seriously, with FW de Klerk choosing to address a meeting in Ventersdorp, Terre'Blanche's home town and stronghold, in 1991. This was considered by those on the far right to be a huge provocation, and resulted in a 2,000-strong protest. As the situation outside the hall where De Klerk was speaking became more and more tense, AWB members opened fire on police, who responded in kind. Three AWB men were killed in the "Battle of Ventersdorp", with six police officers and up to 30 civilians injured.

To some extent Terre'Blanche had forced De Klerk's hand, with the latter calling for a whites-only referendum on the negotiation process. De Klerk famously got his mandate, but this fact, this obvious shift in the political landscape, did not deter Terre'Blanche and his followers.

The AWB's next high-profile act, in 1993, was to raid the World Trade Centre in Kempton Park, where multi-party negotiations were taking place. In a surreal twist, many of the 3,000 AWB men involved brought along their families and their braais. A relaxed atmosphere turned ugly as Terre'Blanche's personal guard, the Ystergarde, became restive and, witnesses say, drunk. Soon enough an armoured car was used to smash through the glass sidings of the centre. Delegates fled in terror as the heavily armed mob moved in, destroying furniture and, as a particularly memorable calling card, urinating throughout the building.

"The white supremacist leader Eugene Terre'Blanche was the biggest threat to the negotiations that ended apartheid in South Africa and established majority rule in 1994. During the transition from apartheid, following the release of Nelson Mandela from prison in 1990, to the general election of 1994, Terre'Blanche gave warning of a civil war in South Africa if white rule were to end. He tried to rally white support by raising fears of a communist regime under Mandela and organised a terrorist campaign to rouse popular Afrikaner support. But he failed to prevent Mandela being elected as the first non-white President of modern South Africa and thereafter his influence and credibility faded. "

– The opening paragraph of Eugène Terre'Blanche's
obituary in The Times of London, 5 April 2010

Still, this was the least of the AWB's crimes. As tensions mounted in the run-up to the 1994 election, the situation in Bophuthatswana became especially tense. Lucas Mangope, the corrupt and autocratic leader of the homeland, had made it clear that, against the wishes of the vast majority of his people, he would ensure Bophuthatswana remained independent of a new democratic South Africa. Eventually, in February 1994, a huge civil-service strike hit the homeland, to the point that even policing stopped. Only the Bophuthatswana army, on the verge of mutiny itself, remained loyal to its government.

Fearing a coup, Mangope invited the Afrikaner Volksfront (AVF) under Constant Viljoen to help prop up his rule. But he specifically requested that the AWB, who he considered overtly racist and hyper-violent, not come. Terre'Blanche didn't care, and he rallied his men to the area. The South African Defence Force then became involved, twice asking Terre'Blanche and his militias to leave. They refused; tensions mounted. "The end of Bophuthatswana was," as legendary news photographer Greg Marinovich later wrote, "clearly imminent."

While negotiations between the Bophuthatswana Defence Force and the paramilitaries went on through the night, 37 people were killed across the homeland, most allegedly by AWB gunmen. The following morning, 11 March 1994, Marinovich was on the scene, along with various international and local reporters and cameramen. The situation had deteriorated to disastrous levels, with AWB members seen openly firing at civilians and into shacks and huts. "*Ons is op 'n kaffirskiet piekniek,*" Marinovich was told by a man drinking beer with his girlfriend on plastic chairs on the back of a bakkie.

It wasn't long before the Bop soldiers, furious at the slaughter, took their revenge. In a notorious scene, footage of which would be relayed around the world, Ontlametse Bernstein Menyatsoe approached three AWB men in their crippled blue Mercedes-Benz. Two had been wounded; one was already dead. The soldier asked "Colonel" Alwyn Wolfaardt whether he and his accomplices were in the AWB. Wolfaardt answered in the affirmative, and begged for his life.

In the later Truth and Reconciliation Commission hearing, Menyatsoe would say that he had witnessed the AWB shooting innocent civilians and that he was highly disturbed. His response to Wolfaardt, as the cameras rolled, was to execute the two surviving men with his assault rifle. Menyatsoe was ultimately granted amnesty by the TRC.

Speaking five years later in London, Marinovich smiled at the memory of that decisive morning in South African and AWB history: "Ja, it was like 'BANG!', end of apartheid!"

But the end of apartheid wasn't quite the end of Terre'Blanche, who turned his increasingly irrelevant attentions to forming a volkstaat for Afrikaners. As his organisation slipped into obscurity, Terre'Blanche himself was unable to restrain his inner jackboot. In 2001, he was sentenced to six years' imprisonment for the attempted murder of Paul Motshabi and the assault of a petrol-pump attendant. Motshabi was left brain damaged, seriously disabled and unable to work. Terre'Blanche served three years.

After a brief attempted revival of the AWB in 2008 in response to crime, the Eskom crisis and rampant corruption, Terre'Blanche was hacked and beaten to death on his farm, allegedly over unpaid wages, in early 2010. It was, in its grimness, classic Terre'Blanche timing, as his murder came at the height of an unpleasant, racially charged few months in which Julius Malema had been exhorting the ANC Youth League's followers to murder farmers. *(See Julius Malema.)* A race war was threatened and widely predicted. But, even in macabre death, the man with the "blue flames" in his "blowtorch eyes" – as described by Jani Allan, the *Sunday Times* columnist with whom he was alleged to have had an affair – was unable to start the war he had predicted.

Once again, this hardy, long-suffering country had survived one of its most unpleasant inhabitants.

Mark Thatcher

b. 15 August 1953

*Son of Margaret Thatcher; one-time Constantia
resident; aspirant arms dealer; coup d'état funder;
representative of the wave of modern Euroscum using
South Africa as a base to run their dubious dealings*

WITH THE CORRUPTION AND GENERAL LAWLESSNESS that persecutes honest, hard-working South Africans, it is to some extent not surprising that criminals are attracted to our country. If you're looking to set up shop in a place where justice can be bought and "administered" on a whim, a country where there is a decent infrastructure (if in decline) and yet there are people in important positions who can be "persuaded", a country where official incompetence is rife and policing is moribund, then certainly South Africa has the right kind of reputation.

That reputation is, however, only half-earned. Sometimes crooks from afar come to South Africa to live the good life and they get way with all kinds of naughtiness. And sometimes they come up against factors that are not so well publicised: our excellent detective work and our superb legal system. In other words, sometimes people think they're coming to a southern African banana republic but, troubled as our magnificent land is, a banana republic it ain't.

Mark Thatcher, son of the former British prime minister, Maggie, moved to Cape Town with his family in 1994 after settling a racketeering case and surviving a criminal charge for tax evasion in Texas (among other legal cases). A failed accountant by trade, Thatcher had regularly made international headlines since the early 1980s, once for getting embarrassingly lost in the Sahara during the Paris-Dakar rally, but mostly for claims that he regularly used his mother's name and influence to further his business career. Most memorably, he was questioned by Britain's parliament after allegedly earning millions of pounds from a British arms deal to Saudi Arabia in 1985 – but nothing had ever quite stuck, and he amassed a good-sized fortune over the years, with a playboy lifestyle to match.

It wasn't too long before, to no-one's surprise, he was causing trouble in South Africa. In 1998 Thatcher was investigated for running a loan-shark operation that lent money to police officers. Interest, apparently, was set at 20 percent. But he took his disrespect of our law and its institutions to a new level altogether when he became involved in the failed coup attempt on Equatorial Guinea in 2004.

At the time "Scratcher" Thatcher, as he is known, had fallen in with some shady characters he was acquainted with via the Old Boy connection, who had their eye on the oil-rich pickings in Equatorial Guinea. With a small mercenary force and some rocket launchers, they figured they could oust the country's brutal dictator of 25 years, Teodoro Obiang Nguema Mbasogo, and land themselves in the money. One of Thatcher's new pals was ex-Etonian Simon Mann, who just happened to live down the road from him in Constantia.

"The morning the Scorpions arrived to arrest him, on August 25, he was asleep and I was working out on the treadmill. When I finished I could hear the water running in the shower. The Scorpions had woken him and allowed him to shower before interrogating him. They had a man standing outside the shower to make sure he didn't do a runner...

He said in his plea bargain that he'd financed the helicopter thinking it would be used as an ambulance and only later had come to suspect it was going to be used for mercenary activities.

Did Simon ask Mark to help or did Mark ask Simon if he could help? To this day, I have no idea if Mark was telling the truth because he wouldn't talk to me about it.

But I think his choice not to pull out when he became suspicious shows his priorities. I think he was incredibly selfish, putting his own needs for self-fulfilment, greed and lust for power before his family...

I feel sorry for him. It's as though he was given one of the best seats at the banquet of life and he's blown it. He's got his money. But I just don't know who he will do his business deals with now.

Who would want to go into business with him? They'd either have to be extremely forgiving or naive or corrupt."

– Extracts from a Daily Mail interview with
Diane Thatcher, ex-wife of Mark, September 2006

It was a ridiculous endeavour from the start; more a boys' spy-game adventure than anything. Thatcher's wife at the time, Diane, even noted that he returned from a business trip reading Frederick Forsyth's *The Dogs of War*, a best-selling 1970s novel about a mercenary-led assault to take over a fictional African state. (Forsyth is believed to have based his research for the book almost entirely on a hypothetical coup of Equatorial Guinea.)

Famously – and predictably – the planned takeover flopped when Mann was arrested in Zimbabwe, along with 69 others, after landing to pick up their weapons supplies. Mann had been the brawn behind the operation, the man on the ground, and he was eventually deported to Equatorial Guinea to languish in what the media uniformly described as the "notorious" Black Beach prison, at Obiang's pleasure.

Thatcher, meanwhile, had provided the logistical support – which might well explain why it all went awry. In August 2004, he was arrested by the Scorpions for contravening the Foreign Military Assistance Act. He had sent money for a helicopter to carry the plotters, which is what ultimately got him into trouble despite his best efforts to convince the bemused judge that he believed it was to be used as an air ambulance. As part of a plea bargain, Thatcher admitted to negligence for investing in an aircraft "without taking proper investigations into what it would be used for". He copped a suspended sentence and a R3 million fine, and left South Africa as quickly as he could.

Yet again, Thatcher had wriggled out of trouble (once again, with the assistance of his doting mother), while Mann and several other plotters suffered the horrors of Black Beach. They were released in 2009; some say after diplomatic pressure from Jacob Zuma, others say because Mann's family paid Obiang a ransom. Mann, an ex-SAS commando, openly claims that Thatcher was intricately involved in the whole affair and is said to remain deeply pissed off with the lies he told.

For what it's worth, Thatcher became, officially, Sir Mark Thatcher, 2nd Baronet on the death of his father in 2003. His murky history of "fixing" and middle-manning suggests him to be the type of person who likes to make people aware of his full title. As such, and taking into account his brief and controversial residency stint in South Africa – he left the country soon after copping his plea – he is the consummate representative of the self-important European "barons" and "marquises" who come to South Africa, particularly the southern suburbs of Cape Town, to swan about in questionably acquired luxury for a few years before having to make a quick getaway in the night. We certainly don't need their type on our shores; or their less affected but more ruthless mafia-style counterparts from the Czech Republic and elsewhere who enjoy the shadier elements of what Johannesburg and its surrounds have to offer.

Thatcher is banned from entering the US. He left South Africa under a cloud, extremely lucky to have avoided jail. In 2005 even Monaco asked him to leave the country, as part of Prince Albert's drive to clear its reputation as a refuge for shady businessmen. Considering the vast oversupply of dodgy Eurotrash quasi-criminal folk in South Africa, we really should be following Monaco's example and giving them all the boot.

Andries Treurnicht

19 February 1921 – 22 April 1993

NG Kerk minister; Minister of Education (1976-1979);
Soweto riots initiator; founder of the Conservative
Party; old-school apartheid advocate

MUCH AS PAUL KRUGER HAD OBSESSED about the *uitlanders*, the expat migrant workers who travelled to the Witwatersrand in the late 1880s to take advantage of the newly discovered gold fields, so the apartheid regime feared something rotten the encroachment of Englishness. In the 1970s, it was clear that English was becoming a lingua franca among black South Africans, and that it was the language of business and commerce. Black children were taught mainly in English or their home language, and this put the wind up the Nats, as ever living in terror of the decay of Afrikaner culture.

The very obvious flourishing of Afrikaans language and culture since 1994, when it was freed of the shackles of what Desmond Tutu termed "the oppressor's language", gives lie to this stunted belief, but one must remember that the nationalist politicians of the time were the children of Boer War commandos and concentration-camp internees. The Afrikaner government was not about to let the English win on any battlefield – even those of the dilapidated schoolrooms of young black South Africans.

Naturally, there was much pressure on this particular matter from the Afrikaner Broederbond, that secretive and less-than-delightful organisation dedicated to the preservation and advancement of Afrikaner interests. Conveniently, they could count among their members many politicians in high places, including, in the early 1970s, one Andries Treurnicht, a previous chair of the Broederbond and current deputy minister of Bantu education.

Dr Treurnicht, an ordained minister and the holder of a political philosophy doctorate from the University of Cape Town, was well aware of his priorities. One figure, for example, holds that for every R100 spent on white schoolchildren in the mid-1970s, approximately R6.50 went to black schoolchildren. His particular response to the great language concern was the implementation of a policy that would see black children taught half in English and half in Afrikaans, a suggestion that was understandably poorly received in the townships. Like it or not, Afrikaans was deeply associated with apartheid, and the law was seen as a deeply humiliating attempt by the state to force a hated language onto the children of the nation already stigmatised by its policy as future "hewers of wood".

But the Nats had pooh-poohed any suggestions of classroom resistance. Punt Janson, who worked under Treurnicht, was asked by opposition MPs if he'd consulted with black people about the decision. His reply was educational: "A black man may be trained to work on a farm or in a factory. He may work for an employer who is either English-speaking or Afrikaans-speaking and the man who has to give him instructions may be either English-speaking or Afrikaans-speaking. Why should we now start quarrelling about the medium of instruction among the black people as well? … No, I have not consulted them and I am not going to consult them."

"This uprising of 1976-77 was, of course, the historic watershed of the period we are reporting about. Within a short period of time, it propelled into the forefront of our struggle millions of young people, thus immeasurably expanding the active forces of the revolution and inspiring other sections of our people into activity…

It brought into our midst comrades, many of whom had very little contact with the ANC, if any. It put at the immediate disposal of our movement militant cadres who were ready and yearning to carry out even the most difficult missions that the movement wished to give them."

– *Oliver Tambo, June 1985*

When it was finalised, the Afrikaans Medium Decree of 1974 stated that Afrikaans be used in the teaching of "mathematics, arithmetic and social studies". The results of this deeply ingrained fear of some kind of cultural decline, some sort of descent into irrelevance, that suffused Afrikaner nationalism were catastrophic. Besides the very obvious logistical difficulty of getting non-fluent teachers to instruct in Afrikaans, which alone would have caused havoc to the Bantu education system, the rebellion was inevitable. Students from various schools in Soweto went on strike and organised secret meetings. A mass rally was proposed for 16 June 1976. Treurnicht's disrespectful and heavy-handed management of an appalling policy was about to meet a wave of unrestrained fury that would radicalise and harden the hearts of an entire generation of young black South Africans.

The rally, estimated to involve up to 10,000 schoolchildren and teachers, went ahead and was met with a wall of policemen. It was intended to be a peaceful event and was generally so until a couple of kids took to throwing stones at the cops. A Colonel Kleingeld allegedly fired the first shot. Schoolboy Hastings Ndlovu, 16, fell dead. There was panic. More shots were fired. Clinics and hospitals were quickly inundated with dying and wounded children. By the end of the day 23 people were dead, among them Hector Pieterson.

There was intense anger after the massacre and the township was flooded with police and army special units. The violence quickly spread, with killing that was at times indiscriminate. Uprisings occurred around the country. As many as 500 people were killed.

The 16th of June 1976 was a day that would ring through the ages, and the iconic image of Hector Pieterson being carried through the streets by a fellow pupil while his distraught sister runs alongside would serve to fuel both the radicalisation of black South Africans and the fire of anti-apartheid sentiment growing around the globe. And all because some frightened, ugly men wanted to impose their sad ideas of racial and cultural superiority onto the children of South Africa.

Treurnicht and the apartheid state had made the classrooms of the 1970s the battlefield of his parents' generation's war. It was unspeakably cruel and utterly unnecessary – but ultimately, and ironically, it proved to be an important milestone in the eventual undoing of white rule.

Treurnicht, of course, took none of the blame. He was a real beaut, the good doctor, and he went on to found the Conservative Party in the 1980s in rebellion against the "liberal" policies of PW Botha. He proved to be such a dinosaur that he campaigned bitterly for the "no" camp in De Klerk's 1992 referendum on the dismantling of apartheid –Dr No, they called him. In the end, he died a year to the month before South Africa's first democratic elections. What a great pity he didn't live to see 1994; he would have gone to his grave knowing he'd been defeated, as he deserved to do.

Manto Tshabalala-Msimang

9 October 1940 – 16 December 2009

Minister of Health (1999-2008); Aids dissenter; beetroot, garlic and lemon lover; Mbeki-appointed "Angel of Death"

JOURNALISTIC ETHICS REQUIRE, QUITE SIMPLY, that you investigate all sides of a story. But sometimes you wonder if there's a point. For example, was Adolf Hitler good at impressions? Did he make children laugh? Sometimes a person's crime can be so vast that it almost seems pointless discussing the other side of the story; ultimately the crime comes, quite rightly, to define the person.

Mantombazana Edmie Tshabalala-Msimang is one such individual. She was certainly no Hitler, but comparisons with the *Führer's* notorious Auschwitz physician Josef Mengele are not without substance. For one, they both abrogated their moral responsibilities to a higher authority; for another, they both earned the sobriquet "Angel of Death". Tshabalala-Msimang was, however, better known as "Dr Beetroot", the South African health minister who denied that HIV causes Aids and instead recommended vegetables, olive oil and other "nutritional" remedies.

But Manto, as she was known but preferred not to be called, had one hell of a back story. Born in 1940, in Durban, she soon ended up at the hotbed of ANC learning, the University of Fort Hare. She graduated in 1961, a year after the Sharpeville massacre and the banning of the ANC by the apartheid state. The ANC then asked her and various other young cadres, including one Thabo Mbeki, to go into exile. They were told to get to Tanzania as best they could and, with little other option, they slipped out of South Africa on foot and walked. They were arrested and held for a while in Northern Rhodesia, but eventually made it.

That's how far back Thabo and Manto went.

Tshabalala-Msimang was soon packed off to Leningrad in the USSR, where she lived and studied medicine, graduating in 1969. Returning to Tanzania as a fluent Russian speaker, she continued her medical studies and her work for the ANC in exile. She learnt Swahili too, and took control of the health and wellbeing of exiled members. She managed to find time to study for a Masters degree in Antwerp, Belgium, graduating in 1980, whereafter she worked in various ANC jobs in Zambia and Botswana.

Manto Tshabalala-Msimang would eventually step onto South African soil again in 1990, nearly three decades after going into exile. She became an MP in 1994 after the first democratic election, and during the Mandela presidency she was chairwoman of the health portfolio committee. When Mbeki became president in 1999, she was elevated to the position of health minister – and that's when the trouble started.

Tshabalala-Msimang, who was schooled amid the high drama and paranoia of the Cold War, who spent seven formative years in exile in the USSR convinced an assassin's bullet was imminent, had learnt much. She was highly educated and was most certainly not stupid, a fact that made her future actions that much more deplorable – because ultimately she would value blind loyalty over rational and ethical decision-making. And she was loyal, to the death, to Thabo Mbeki.

"Raw garlic and a skin of the lemon – not only do they give you a beautiful face and skin but they also protect you from disease."
    – Manto Tshabalala-Msimang, 2005

"In the past we had a government that killed people; now we have one that lets them die."
    – Pieter Dirk-Uys

Her reign as health minister was a catastrophic squandering of potential, and a defining failure of the Mbeki years. *(See Thabo Mbeki.)* On so many fronts, time was against South Africa and yet there was, at best, a lack of urgency in everything Mbeki did. At worst, there was murderous negligence, and it was Tshabalala-Msimang's role as the executor of Mbeki's policies on HIV/Aids that epitomised this belief in much of the South African public.

As such, and with much vigour, she squandered nine crucial years to act against the Aids pandemic. She spent large amounts of this time fighting the Treatment Action Campaign (TAC) in court, desperately trying to stop the roll-out of antiretroviral drugs (ARVs) that lengthen and normalise the lives of those with HIV and reduce mother-to-child transmissions. The rest of the time, she punted the crackpot ideas of notorious snake-oil salesman Matthias Rath, a vitamin peddler and vocal denier of the link between HIV and Aids. She also spoke out loudly about how proper nutrition would stop the wave of HIV, suggesting that regular doses of garlic, African potatoes, lemons, olive oil and, of course, beetroot, would keep people healthy.

At the time many people in South Africa laughed, but when it became clear what was happening to people in poor and rural communities, the laughter stopped and the outrage grew.

In an ugly interview with John Robbie on Talk Radio 702 in 2000, Tshabalala-Msimang refused to say that she believed HIV causes Aids, but such was the brouhaha that eventually the cabinet, in 2002, released a statement admitting that it does. Mbeki chose not speak on the matter again, and it was left to his health minister to continue his obscure policies and retard all efforts to implement modern medical antidotes to the pandemic.

Tshabalala-Msimang stuck closely to Mbeki's theme, motivated by deep racial paranoia, that if the government addressed poverty among blacks generally as opposed to HIV and Aids specifically, then the problem would go away. Unfortunately, with as many as 30 percent of the population, or 5.5 million people, infected with the virus by 2005, the policy was plain wrong, and her prevarications and excuses simply held no water.

In 2003 she claimed the cost of providing ARVs would imperil the delivery of healthcare generally in South Africa. However, a report suggested that such was the burden of HIV-related illness on the healthcare system that an ARV roll-out would actually save the government money. Tshabalala-Msimang tried to bury the report, but it was eventually leaked and the government's hand was forced; ARVs were to be made widely available to the public.

But even then there was a complete lack of will on the matter, and though she cannily adapted her public utterances to merge mainstream and dissenting outlooks on HIV/Aids, Tshabalala-Msimang refused to reverse her personal opinions. Condemnation of her and government health policies were global and deeply embarrassing for South Africa. In 2006 she was famously criticised at the International Aids Conference in Toronto for providing a South African stand that was, in effect, a vegetable display; the UN's envoy on HIV described her as part of a "lunatic fringe", while her policies were "obtuse, dilatory, and negligent". Eighty-one leading HIV scientists subsequently signed a document asking Mbeki to dismiss her.

As recently as 2008, doctors at Manguzi Hospital in KwaZulu-Natal – the South African and possibly world epicentre of the HIV crisis – were being censured for providing pregnant mothers with dual-therapy ARV treatments (paid for through international funding). Around the same time, health ministry-organised "HIV information workshops", which Tshabalala-Msimang attended and even addressed, were still welcoming Aids denialists and dissenters while excluding TAC members. Literature for these events was invariably provided by the Matthias

Rath Foundation.

Manto, it is widely said, was not a particularly nice person. She was rude, dismissive and egotistical. Vindictive to the end, she conspired to have Deputy Minister of Health Nozizwe Madlala-Routledge fired by Mbeki in 2007. The two women had clashed repeatedly, particularly over Madlala-Routledge's widely acclaimed efforts to end the government's Aids denialism, and Tshabalala-Msimang had had enough of being shown up. "I'll get you," she reportedly told her deputy not long before the sacking, yet another shameful episode in her disastrous reign.

The last few years of Tshabalala-Msimang's life descended into sickness and personal controversy. The South African minister of health underwent a liver transplant in 2007, news that the government tried to suppress. Not long afterwards, the *Sunday Times* ran a story detailing how, during a hospital stay for a shoulder operation in 2005, she had ordered hospital staff to buy her whiskey and wine. Questions were inevitably asked about the nature of her liver problems, with widespread speculation within the medical fraternity implying that her liver had failed due to alcoholism and that she may have been illegitimately promoted up the donor lists. A week later the same newspaper exposed how Tshabalala-Msimang had stolen from patients while working in a hospital in Botswana during her exile. There was fury in the ANC, but no charges were ever brought against the paper, strongly suggesting that the *Sunday Times*'s headline "Manto: A Drunk And A Thief" was indeed true.

Tshabalala-Msimang's career fizzled out along with her health. When the ANC recalled Mbeki in 2008, Barbara Hogan assumed her position as health minister to great jubilation in many circles. There was literally singing in the streets on the day of the announcement. After the 2009 elections, Manto was removed from cabinet altogether; by then she was an Mbeki-ite in Zuma's time, unloved and unwanted. She died of complications related to her transplant in December 2009. Cynical observers noted that she clearly hadn't been eating enough garlic and beetroot.

Tshabalala-Msimang was undeniably a vital cog in the struggle to free South Africa, a heroine in many ways to many people. But the sad truth is that she sent 300,000 or more South Africans to an early grave and allowed countless young children to be infected by their mothers by perpetuating the catastrophic health policies and batty pseudoscience of Thabo Mbeki. Yes, Mbeki was ultimately responsible, but Tshabalala-Msimang, his minion at the coalface, could see and understand the damage being done. She was simply too cowardly, too bereft of sympathy and moral strength, to do the right thing. She failed South Africa gravely when it needed her most. Does her response to HIV define Tshabalala-Msimang? Sadly, there are more than 300,000 reasons to say yes.

Jan van Riebeeck

21 April 1619 – 18 January 1677

VOC official; Commander of the Cape (1652-1662);
founder of Cape Town; founding father of the Afrikaner
nation; fraudster; deliverer of rudimentary apartheid
principles to South Africa

In the 1600s, as far as Europeans were concerned, southern Africa was a huge area that merely got in the way of trade between Europe and the East. As a result, white folk had stopped off only briefly before 1652.

In 1488 the Portuguese explorer Bartholomeu Dias rounded the Cape of Good Hope. Not only was he tasked with finding the sea route to India, but also, in a mission that illustrates how unenlightened the times were, with locating the mythical kingdom of Prester John, the generous and virtuous ruler of a legendary eastern Christian land surrounded by Muslims and pagans.

Dias got as far as the Bushman's River mouth, near today's Kenton-on-Sea, erecting a cross and then returning to Portugal after his crew told him in no uncertain terms that an onward voyage to India was out of the question. His successor, Vasco da Gama, was altogether harsher (he is recorded as being unspeakably cruel), and he passed Dias's cross on 16 December 1497. That Christmas, Da Gama anchored in a pretty harbour, naming it "Natal" in honour of the birth of Christ, before continuing on to reach India, thus opening the crucial sea route linking Europe and the East.

A century later, in 1602, the Dutch East India Company – the *Vereenigde Oost-Indische Compagnie*, or VOC – came into being in response to the failure of Portuguese traders to meet the demand for spices, especially for black pepper, in northern Europe. The Portuguese had pretty much dominated the trade throughout the 1500s, but now the British and the Dutch were waking up. The VOC would go on to become the first company to offer stocks and shares, effectively the world's first multinational corporation and one of the most influential companies in history. Not only was it a mandated monopoly, but to cover the significant risks involved in sea trade it could establish colonies, raise armies and police forces, issue money and even wage wars. It was very much a sub-contraction of the ugly

"WELL, THERE GOES THE NEIGHBOURHOOD!"

and expensive business of empire, which perhaps the colonising state's treasury preferred not to sponsor. In this liberalised manner, the VOC acted on behalf of the Netherlands, paying a hefty dividend to the state.

The scale of the VOC's endeavour is, even in today's globalised world, hugely impressive. In 200 years a million Europeans were despatched across the globe on 4,800 ships on behalf of the colonising endeavours of the company. Eventually it would all collapse, one of the many reasons being the poor salaries paid to its staff, which absolutely guaranteed widespread and crippling corruption.

Indeed, a company man by the name of Johan Anthoniszoon van Riebeeck, who had served in Batavia (now Jakarta), Japan and Tonking (in modern Vietnam), was recalled to the Netherlands when he was unlucky enough to be caught trading for himself. He probably felt his career with the company was over, but for a spot of luck on the way home: the boat stopped for a few days in the lee of a beautiful mountain and harbour at the Cape of Good Hope, and Van Riebeeck, like many others before him, noted that it was a temperate and fertile area.

The VOC subsequently chose him, in 1651, to establish a small but permanent refuelling station and hospital for company ships at this very spot. The indigenous folk of what would become South Africa were about to be colonised by a corporation. On 6 April 1652, the *Drommedaris*, *Reijger* and *Goede Hoop* landed at what would become Cape Town, completely and utterly changing the future of South Africa and robbing its indigenous people of the freedom to shape their own lives for 342 years.

Ironically, the VOC had no imperial ambitions in South Africa; the base was simply there to provide shelter, fresh food and water for passing VOC ships. But despite an initially successful trade that saw the Dutch bartering copper and tobacco for livestock, conflict with the local Khoi population was inevitable. After a hard first winter, Van Riebeeck set about building a fort on what is now the Parade in Cape Town's CBD and established the Company Gardens nearby and a farm further south. (Work on the Castle only began in 1666, after his departure.) Demands on the settlement from passing ships were huge, and farming operations expanded fast, pushing the Khoi off land they had known for countless generations. They rose up violently against settlers in 1659, initiating the First Khoikhoi-Dutch War, but were put down and forced to retreat further into the interior.

In the meantime, the arrival of settlers from Europe and slaves from the East was steadily increasing. Van Riebeeck persuaded the VOC to allow him to release a number of company employees as *vrijeburghers*, or free citizens, to farm commercially along the slopes of Table Mountain. Thus, a classic VOC-styled racial hierarchy had formed within a matter of years: company servants at the top, then free burghers, then slaves, then the "natives". Sound familiar? (In a chilling portrait of things to come, Van Riebeeck even banished people to Robben Island.)

By the time Van Riebeeck left the Cape in 1662, there were about 130 VOC officials, a few European women and children, and at least 180 slaves living in the burgeoning settlement. In 1688, the first boatload of persecuted French Huguenots landed in the Cape, and the white man was in Africa for good.

And thus was the die cast for South Africa. Van Riebeeck may not have been the grand colonialist, the man with the big ideas, but he was the thin end of the wedge. Slavery, the theft of land, the rape of resources, the violent repression of indigenous people and the total exclusion of blacks from any form of a non-subservient existence arrived in South Africa with Jan van Riebeeck.

"Van Riebeeck left the Cape in 1662 understanding that his original idea of an intensive settlement had failed."

– Hermann Giliomee, historian

It is difficult to apportion blame to the man personally. The company fraudster who found himself at the bottom of Africa almost by default simply attempted to do what was expected of him. (Ironically, in effectively establishing a growing colony, he ultimately concluded that he'd failed in completing his task of maintaining a small and contained settlement.) Nonetheless, that is his legacy, and Jan van Riebeeck has gone on to take his place in history as the founding father of modern South Africa, and in particular of the Afrikaner nation. Of course, the VOC was the real big daddy.

Marthinus van Schalkwyk

b. 10 November 1959

Former NNP leader; former leader of the opposition; former Premier of the Western Cape; current Minister of Tourism; permanently discredited political hypocrite

DEMOCRACY IS, TO ITS CORE, FRUSTRATING, flawed and difficult. It's the least bad system of government. It's like that because it's about people and how they feel, and in South Africa that can make things very complicated. Firstly, we are – to use an unavoidable cliché – the Rainbow Nation, a collection of different peoples with countless different outlooks. Secondly, and equally unavoidably given our past, a great many people are angry. A great many are poorly educated. The majority get their news and information from the laughably politicised SABC, while a wealthy few live in ignorance as self-imposed and as cloistered as their Tuscan villa at Deja Vu Lifestyle Estate, Fourways.

It is in this environment that politicians in the democratic state have to operate, and it's hard, given the circumstances, to change voters' allegiances. Still, this might explain why, after living a life that would strongly suggest a deep distaste for the idea of true democracy, Marthinus "Kortbroek" van Schalkwyk treated our new democratic institutions with such disregard that he all but proved the thesis.

Van Schalkwyk may have been happier had he been born twenty years earlier, but as it was he arrived in what was then Pietersburg in 1959. He finished school in 1977, went off to the Rand Afrikaans University and picked up a taste for politics, leading, rather harmlessly, the Student Representative Council. But then he went on to chair the Afrikaner Studentebond, a kind of Broederbond youth league. This was not a pretty organisation, and Van Schalkwyk's involvement marks his taste for Afrikaner nationalism and the ideas of the Broederbond in general.

The Broederbond, lest we forget, was at the heart of the apartheid state. It *was* apartheid, with a chairman once saying that it was born out of "the deep conviction that the Afrikaner volk has been planted in this country by the hand of God, destined to survive as a separate volk with its own calling". This is the organisation that Jan Smuts aptly decried as "dangerous", "cunning" and "fascist". (The Afrikaner Studentebond, incidentally, had been formed in 1933 – a good

year for fascism if we're honest – when Afrikaans students broke away from the National Union of Students in protest at the admission of black students.)

Van Schalkwyk went on to be a founding member and chairman of an organisation known as Jeugkrag. It painted itself as a moderate organisation for Afrikaner youngsters interested neither in the right wing nor the left. Purportedly liberal, it was designed to foster dialogue between young people of all races and backgrounds, and it met with senior ANC figures long before the unbanning of the ANC. And yet Jeugkrag was a blatant attempt by the apartheid state to subvert the work being done in organisations such as The Institute for Democracy in South Africa (Idasa). It turned out, ultimately, that Van Schalkwyk was working for military intelligence. Just how much he was involved in its creation as a subversive arm of the apartheid state has never been established.

> "They [NNP leaders] are after a few more perks. They are going wherever they think they will get rewards and positions. They have no principles whatsoever."
> – *Helen Suzman, commenting on Van Schalkwyk's decision to merge the NNP into the ANC in 2004*

It figures, however, that this conniving wimp would continue his career in the same vein. He associated himself with FW de Klerk, and eventually went on to lead the New National Party, from 1997. In the 1999 election, the party garnered just 6.9 percent of the vote (versus 20 percent in 1994). Van Schalkwyk then entered into a series of calamitous alliances, at first with the Democratic Party and then, to the horror of his million or so voters, with the ANC. Support for the NNP plummeted to just 1.9 percent in the 2004 general election. Soon afterwards, perhaps feeling the first gusts of the chill wind of a life out of politics, Van Schalkwyk announced that he would merge the NNP with the ANC. In doing so, he essentially handed control of the Western Cape to the ANC, despite this being very clearly against the intentions of the people of the province, as was later borne out by elections.

Still, Van Schalkwyk probably didn't care. He got a junior ministry, an official car and all the rest, and he got to be where the big decisions are made. Kind of. Anyway, Kortbroek had never really given a damn about democracy, had he? Which is to say that Van Schalkwyk is a living, breathing example of the worst kind of self-serving, toadying empty vessel. He blows with the wind, fighting the ideas of the ANC all his life, then chuckling away with Mbeki and Zuma. The man is an invertebrate, a political jellyfish. That a person of his calibre could weasel his way into our current cabinet says a lot, unfortunately, about the state of our democracy.

Hendrik Verwoerd

8 September 1901 – 6 September 1966

Prime Minister of South Africa (1958-1966); social engineer; architect of apartheid; destroyer of "Bantu Education"; embracer of pariah-dom; Mandela's jailer; figure of international and local scorn and loathing

DIE BURGER PROBABLY FELT IT WAS speaking for the nation when it asked, with a woeful heart, that "the God in whom we believe make clear to us in his own time what this horrible event is to signify to our country and her people. Now, we cannot fathom it". The sense that something dreadful had happened was given much succour when more than 250,000 people attended the funeral of Hendrik Frensch Verwoerd, South Africa's slain prime minister, in September of 1966. This man, it was clear, was more than a politician. He was the father of the nation, and he had been taken too soon.

The extent to which so many white South Africans were complicit in the crime of apartheid is perfectly illustrated by *Die Burger*'s editorial and the astonishing attendance at Verwoerd's state funeral. It was a time of great national mourning – for one section of the population, at least.

Interestingly, given his unyielding vision for the future of the country, Verwoerd was not born in South Africa. He did, however, get the next best option, the Netherlands, and his family moved to South Africa a couple of years later, in 1903, in support of the Afrikaner nation after the war. So he was well schooled in the injustices and challenges facing the volk.

Verwoerd was, it appears, something of an academic genius – an evil genius in the making, if you will – winning scholarships and achieving a cum-laude doctorate in philosophy from the University of Stellenbosch before furthering his studies at various universities abroad. Whether Verwoerd was influenced by Nazi racial ideology during his time in Germany in the mid-1920s has never been established, but he certainly showed good form before the Nats assumed power in 1948.

In 1936 he spoke out against the arrival in South Africa of Jews fleeing Hitler, believing they would compete directly with Afrikaner professionals. (Nothing to do with their Jewishness, you see.) Then, once war in Europe had broken out, he vehemently opposed South Africa's siding with the Allies. From 1937, he edited *Die Transvaler*, which displayed strong pro-Nazi sympathies during the most destructive war the world had ever seen, something *The Star* in Johannesburg accused him of. He sued, but the judge agreed that *Die Transvaler* was essentially a conduit for pro-Nazi propaganda.

In 1948, delighted by the triumph of Afrikaner nationalism under DF Malan, Verwoerd stepped down from the newspaper and entered the senate. *(See DF Malan.)* Two years later he was in the cabinet, having risen to the position of minister of native affairs.

Verwoerd was to die, stabbed to death in parliament, in 1966, having been elected prime minister in 1958. He only ever held the two offices, and he made them his life's work. In those 16 years in senior office, Verwoerd would pen and preside over some of the most oppressive legislation imaginable – he is known as the architect of apartheid with good reason. His party had campaigned openly on the ticket, even using the word "apartheid". It promised to legislate huge barriers between black and white people. Apartness it would be, and Verwoerd would be its greatest, surest advocate.

The simplest way to deal with Verwoerd is to look at his legislation. Apartheid, after all, was a collection of laws, and Verwoerd was their driving force. By the time he assumed his cabinet position in 1950, the Nats had already passed the Prohibition of Mixed Marriages Act in 1949. He quickly added the Immorality Act, which banned sexual relations between black and white people, a thought that must have horrified him and his fellow party members. In the modern world the notion that what happens in people's bedrooms is a concern for the state is virtually inconceivable, but Verwoerd was just getting going.

He believed that South Africa was not a nation, but a collection of nations defined by their race. In order to create these nations, the respective races had to be defined in legislation, which he did via the Population Registration Act of 1950. Suddenly, South Africa was officially a country of Whites, Indians, Coloureds and Blacks. The latter category was further split up into eight ethnic subdivisions, each of which was to be assigned a "homeland", for example KwaZulu or the Transkei, of which members of each division would then become citizens – even if they'd never been there in their lives.

The Group Areas Act, passed in the same year, then consolidated Verwoerd's official racial classifications by demarcating exactly where people could live. This was grand apartheid at its worst, and chances are that, if you are living in South Africa today, where you live is still defined by your race, and was effectively decided six decades ago by Mr Verwoerd. Such was the impact of Verwoerd, that geographical apartness still defines South African life, still scars our landscape and still divides our people.

And it was tough if you found yourself living in the wrong area. Entire communities were uprooted and destroyed. Sophiatown was cleared, as was District Six. Indians were removed from Johannesburg and dumped in Fordsburg; removed from downtown Pietermaritzburg and dumped in Northdale. Blacks were sent far away to the South Western Townships. It was astonishing and appalling social re-engineering. The vice grip of the apartheid government had been ruthlessly and systematically applied, but it wasn't yet the end of the astounding legislative onslaught on the black people of South Africa.

"'A disaster,' said an opposition newspaper, the *Cape Times*, of Verwoerd's appointment, and in the black slum townships ringing the South African cities, the reaction ranged from explosive resentment to dismay. Yet Hendrik Verwoerd is no simple, Kaffir-bashing white supremacist. Born in The Netherlands, he was brought to South Africa as an infant by his grocer father. A fiery Nationalist from the start, he graduated from the Afrikaans-speaking Stellenbosch University, continued his studies in Germany. Returning to South Africa as a professor in 1927, he married lively Betsy Schoombee, who boasts that none of their seven children was ever bathed or put to bed by a native servant...

Under Verwoerd, South Africa will continue to stand alone on its continent as the only nation or colony that does not offer even a pretense of democratic rights to its black citizens. But Verwoerd remains supremely confident that his is the only way to keep whites in Africa from drowning in a black sea. 'In South Africa,' he proclaimed last week, 'we are being carried forward as never before by the overwhelming current of inspired nationalism which has taken hold of our people. There are forces that are unconquerable. This is one of them.'"

– Extract taken from a Time magazine profile
of Verwoerd, titled "God's Man", published shortly
after he was appointed prime minister, September 1958

Communism was banned. Coloureds were banned from the voting roll. Blacks were banned from performing skilled work in White areas. The minister of native affairs – Verwoerd – was awarded the right to boot Blacks off private or public land and establish resettlement camps. Blacks were required to carry pass books at all times; without a pass, a black person could do little more than stay in the countryside.

Just four years into the nightmare that was the National Party government, Verwoerd had created the building blocks of a bizarre and twisted image of his dream – a whites-only, Afrikaans-led republic that would one day be free of troublesome natives and meddlesome British.

Verwoerd's catastrophic programme of social engineering was far from over, however. In a crime of lasting and monumental proportions, he penned and promulgated the 1953 Bantu Education Act. There is no better person than Verwoerd himself to articulate how he felt about the education of black people. "There is no place for [blacks] in the European community above the level of certain forms of labour," he declared. "What is the use of teaching the Bantu child mathematics when it cannot use it in practice? That is quite absurd. Education must train people in accordance with their opportunities in life, according to the sphere in which they live."

> "Oh yes. You see, one does not have the problem of worrying whether one perhaps could be wrong."
>
> *– Hendrik Verwoerd, on being asked
> by a reporter whether he slept well at night*

Blacks were, as he put it, destined to be "hewers of wood and drawers of water". In a stroke, Verwoerd had stolen the opportunity of a better life from them, and by the 1970s black schools enjoyed one tenth, perhaps even one fifteenth, of the funding of white schools. With a Bantu education behind you, no hard work, no "try and try and try again" would ever get you anywhere near the top. For all the terrible society-transforming legislation that Verwoerd passed in his time, the education system he decreed on generations of South African blacks remains, even today, one of the most damaging aspects of his legacy.

Naturally, the madness of apartheid fomented widespread anger and resentment. Offensive and discriminatory racial practices had, to a greater or lesser degree, been taking place in South Africa pretty much since the moment Van Riebeeck set up shop in 1652 *(see Jan van Riebeeck)*, but there had at least been ways to live around them, to make them tolerable. Verwoerd's vision was all-encompassing, his laws uncompromising; he was the devil who even served the coffee cold, and he wholly redefined the way people lived in South Africa.

The *dompas*, in particular, provided a daily humiliation, an enforced subservience to the South African Police and the white baas. On 21 March 1960, the Pan Africanist Congress (PAC) organised a protest against the pass laws in the township of Sharpeville. Somewhere between 5,000 and 20,000 people pitched on the day – 5,000 peaceful marchers, according to the organisers and eyewitnesses; 20,000 violent protesters, according to the police. Either way, it ended in tragedy. The police gunned down 69 people, including women and children, and injured hundreds more, many shot in the back while fleeing.

It was a watershed, as Nelson Mandela would make clear during his treason trial in 1962. "Government violence can do only one thing and that is to breed counter-violence," he said. "We have warned repeatedly that the government, by resorting continually to violence, will breed in this country counter-violence among the people till ultimately if there is no dawning of sanity on the part of the government, the dispute between the government and my people will finish up by being settled in violence and by force."

Verwoerd knew it, and he responded to black fury and to the marches and the demonstrations against what the police had done that day at Sharpeville by declaring a state of emergency and by arresting tens of thousands of people. Within weeks the ANC and PAC were both banned. International outrage was enormous – far greater than the government had predicted. Five thousand protestors gathered outside the South African embassy in London. Condemnation for apartheid South Africa came from all quarters, even from the racially segregated US.

But Verwoerd, utterly sure in his convictions, was content simply to retreat into the laager. Later in the year, he rigged a plebiscite on the creation of a republic by lowering the voting age to include a young Afrikaner demographic; he won with a 52 percent mandate, created his republic and took South Africa out of the Commonwealth. South Africa would remain stuck in his laager until 1990.

On 6 September 1966 Hendrik Verwoerd was stabbed to death in Cape Town by a deranged parliamentary messenger who would later explain that he was obeying the orders of a giant tapeworm living in his stomach. Dimitri Tsafendas was declared mad and spent the rest of his life in prison, but the ironic – or fitting – story behind the story was that his animosity for Verwoerd had been born of the man's very own laws. Tsafendas, classified as a White, had fallen in love with a coloured woman, but had been legally prevented from living with her. He blamed Verwoerd for his predicament, and his despair and outrage eventually manifested itself in the carefully planned assassination. There was further irony in the fact that Tsafendas had written to the state requesting to be classified as Coloured, and in doing so had alerted authorities to his illegal presence in the country. An order for his deportation had been issued less than a month before Verwoerd's death, but it had not yet been served.

By the time of the architect of apartheid's brutal death, Mandela and co were crushing rocks on Robben Island, the ANC was in exile and a state of civil war

existed between the white and black people of this country. It was some legacy –
celebrated by some, railed against by most. So perhaps certain newspapers of the
country lamented his death, but surely most South Africans felt nothing but relief.
Verwoerd casts the longest of shadows over South Africa, and will do so for years
to come.

BJ Vorster

13 December 1915 – 10 September 1983

Prime Minister (1966-1978) and State President of
South Africa (1978-1979); iconic apartheid sustainer

TURN BACK THE PAGE AND YOU HAVE A MONSTER. A real fire-breathing, laser-eyed beast from the bowels of the beyond. In Balthazar Johannes Vorster you have, well, also a monster. But he doesn't hold a candle to Verwoerd. He is Barney the Dinosaur to Verwoerd's Balrog of Moria.

The problem, among a collection of the fifty most deleterious people in the history of South Africa, is variety. By rights, these pages should be packed from cover to cover with a noisome collection of apartheid administrators, generals and flunkies, give or take a Shaka, Rhodes or Mbeki. In the utilitarian sense of how much damage they did to the people of this country, these guys are at the head of the pack. But for the sake of sanity and proportional representation – big in the South Africa of today – we've spread the love-hate. So the apartheid icons are included: Malan the pioneer, Verwoerd the foundation, Botha the damaging opportunity foregoer. And the minions are represented, too: Basson as the mental sickness of it, De Kock as its brutal enforcer. But there's just no space, or stomach, for them all.

And Vorster? He's here because anyone who was the leader of apartheid South Africa for 12 years deserves a spot. He may not have been as revolutionary as Malan, as ruthless as Verwoerd or as beset by controversy and ill decision-making as Botha, but in BJ Vorster we have the symbol of all those steady contributors to the vision of Afrikaner nationalism that shackled the country for four decades and suppressed the majority of its people – because Vorster was a sustainer of apartheid.

Before stepping into the role of prime minister on Verwoerd's death, he had fulfilled all the necessary requirements: the Nazi sympathies, the Ossewabrandwag membership, the anti-communist and anti-liberal sentiments, the necessary years as minister of justice. But in his role as prime minister he actually took something of a cautious step back from the extremities of the Verwoerd era. He was more charming and approachable than his predecessor; he relaxed rigid

sports segregation, allowed black ambassadors into the country, made reparations between the Afrikaans and English communities, and attempted to cultivate better diplomatic relationships with South Africa's neighbours. It was enough, at least, to appease for much of his tenure the international pressure that had begun to rise since Sharpeville.

Which is all to say that he was an inspired choice for merrily maintaining the apartheid status quo. (Who knows what would have happened if Verwoerd hadn't been murdered? 1994 might have come ten years earlier.) As a result, under Vorster's moniker here, we can include all the unthinking drones who did likewise but are missing from these pages: those other infamous players such as Strijdom and Dönges and the various presidents; the many law-makers; the ministers of defence, Bantu education, native affairs, law and order and the like; the state-security council members; the police commissioners – and on and on and on. Vorster was all these people and more.

Snuki Zikalala

b. 12 May 1951

*Ex-MD of SABC News and Current Affairs; Mbeki
fan; Stalin fan; censorship fan; destroyer of the public
broadcaster's last vestiges of independence*

PERHAPS THE WARNING WAS THERE, in his CV. Snuki Zikalala learnt his version of
the trade of journalism at a Soviet university in Sofia, Bulgaria, deep in the Eastern
Bloc. That right there should have got the alarm bells ringing.

Zikalala is another man steeped in the struggle, another returnee from exile
and communist influence. The struggle for winning freedom and democracy in
South Africa was one thing, but actually doing democracy is another altogether,
as Zikalala would find out.

Zikalala started as head of news at the South African Broadcasting Corporation
in April 2004, exactly ten years into South Africa's democratic age. His position
was one of enormous reach and power. The SABC, lest we forget, wields eighteen
radio stations and four TV channels, three of which are free-to-air. Most South
Africans are unable to afford satellite news from the BBC, Sky or even Al Jazeera.
Most South Africans live out of range of independent radio, such as Talk Radio
702 or 567 Cape Talk. So for the great majority of us, the SABC is the only news
source we will ever receive. Add that to a widespread lack of understanding of how
democratic institutions work and the nature of what democracy means, brought
on by the still-real effects of Bantu Education, and it's clear just how crucial the
SABC is in forming opinions.

Sadly, Zikalala was to set about creating a propaganda machine that would not
just trumpet the pro-ANC agenda, but would specifically look after and protect his
master and president, Thabo Mbeki. Zikalala was, it almost goes without saying,
an Mbeki acolyte. He was once described, rather marvellously, by the late *Mail &
Guardian* columnist Robert Kirby: "He smiles obsequiously and exudes something
even stickier than glycerine." Indeed, evening after evening, SABC *News* viewers
would be subjected to the image of Miranda Strydom leading the top story of the
day about a glorious speech the president had made somewhere. This was more
the GCIS* than the news. But it was the news as Zikalala saw it.

Under his guidance, the SABC very seldom reported on deeply troubling societal issues such as HIV/Aids and crime; newsreaders were, in fact, instructed not to lead bulletins with a crime story. And it brooked no criticism of the ANC, the president or his ministers. When Deputy President Phumzile Mlambo-Ngcuka was booed at a rally in 2005, the SABC refused to broadcast the footage. A documentary on how Thabo Mbeki had come to power was quashed for having elements that were considered unfit for broadcast – which is to say, it included some constructive criticism.

> "The big influence there [in exile in Bulgaria] was the Communist Party. The ruling party must control the way people think. That's the school of thought that he [Zikalala] comes from."
> – *Moeletsi Mbeki, commenting on the blacklisting scandal*

But perhaps Zikalala's greatest crime was to compile a blacklist of political commentators whose thoughts were, he felt, counter-revolutionary, anti-ANC or anti-Mbeki, and who were subsequently banned from appearing on SABC radio or TV programmes. When the *Sowetan* broke the story, the SABC naturally did its best to deny the allegation, but it had the carpet pulled out from under it when veteran radio man John Perlman confirmed that the blacklist was real during a 2006 broadcast of his morning show on its SAfm radio station. (Perlman resigned shortly after being given a verbal warning for his on-air actions.)

An independent commission of enquiry into the blacklist affair established varied motives for people being banned from the public broadcaster's airwaves, and discovered how far removed from legitimate journalism the productions at the SABC had become.

Karima Brown, *Business Day*'s erstwhile political editor and a former ANC activist, was banned for asking difficult questions – "spreading untruths" was how Zikalala was said to have described it. Pious Ncube, the Zimbabwean archbishop, was banned from commenting on what was happening in Zimbabwe. So was Trevor Ncube, the Zimbabwean owner of the *Mail & Guardian*. Moeletsi Mbeki, the president's younger brother, was banned for his regular criticism of the government and South Africa's BEE policies. Paula Slier, the veteran reporter

---

* That's Government Communication and Information System, if you weren't aware. The actual GCIS is "responsible for communication between government and the people". No-one really knows what it was doing while Zikalala was in charge of the SABC.

in the Middle East, was referred to as "that little Jewish girl" and was banned for allegedly being too pro-Israel. The report noted this comment from Zikalala: "From the movement where I come from, we support the PLO".

As the Zuma/Mbeki showdown gathered momentum in 2007, it was, for SABC-watchers, almost amusing to witness the public broadcaster flail about as it tried to work out how to report on what was going on. The corporation was pro-Mbeki, and yet the ANC was rapidly turning pro-Zuma. In the run-up to the event Mbeki was interviewed on fifteen SABC stations; Zuma on exactly none. You could almost see the hand-wringing as the propaganda machine had to deal with increasingly serious fallout for its master, and there was little surprise when it all came crashing down.

Zikalala's suspension by group CEO Dali Mpofu in May 2008 was quickly matched by the counter-suspension of Mpofu by the SABC board. The corporation veritably ground to a standstill as the quagmire of politically motivated warring was resolved, and it took a full year before Zikalala was sent on his way. He left, he claimed, with his head held high, even while his demoralised staff, the (new) SABC board, media watchdogs, various political parties and the public in general celebrated his departure.

But by then the damage was done. Not forgetting the general incompetence that had befallen the SABC under Zikalala's reign – his satellite-TV brainchild, SABC International, lost astronomical amounts of money – in a few short years the public broadcaster had reverted to what it was pre-1994: the mouthpiece of the ruling party. The ANC and its appointees in Auckland Park had become, it seems, content with carrying on the fine tradition of lies, propaganda and mismanagement started by the apartheid state, and it is difficult to see the SABC shaking off this reputation any time in the near future.

Zikalala, like any head of news who had gone before him in the corporation's history, could have been great. He could have taken the broadcaster across a Rubicon of its own. He didn't, and the people it hurts most are mainly poor and black – the people who rely on the SABC for their news-gathering. Zikalala struck a blow for Stalinism by keeping ordinary people ignorant of the truth, and tried to establish a kind of ghastly Ministry of Truth in which he played the role of Big Brother. But for the colour of his skin, he would have done well under Vorster or Botha. Shame on you, Snuki.

Jacob Zuma

b. 12 April 1942

President of South Africa; struggle veteran; trial veteran; husband of many; father of more; charmer; womaniser; appalling moral role model; political appeaser; the Nero of South Africa?

THEY SAY THAT JACOB ZUMA IS a deeply charming man. He is personable, amusing and really does have the common touch. He is able to reach across great yawning chasms of class, race, education and upbringing to make pretty much anyone, of any background, feel at ease, be they white businessmen or foreign dignitaries. And yet, in the history of South Africa, there has probably not been a man more of the people than Jacob Gedleyihlekisa Zuma.

JZ, as he probably doesn't mind being known, was born in 1942 in Nkandla, deep in one of the most beautiful parts of the country. Nkandla is at the heart of Zulu history and culture, and the Warhol-green hills roll into the heat haze seemingly forever, accompanied by the shrill of grasshoppers driven frenzied in the intense heat of a Zululand summer.

Of course, Zuma's childhood was not as idyllic as his surrounds might have suggested. His father, a policeman, died when he was young, leaving his mother to commute to the suburbs of Durban, where she was a domestic worker. Money was scarce and the young Jacob received no formal schooling at all. As he later described it, "There was no chance of me getting educated. I wanted to be a teacher, a priest or a lawyer but all I could do was to try to get other children to show me what they learnt at school." By the age of 15, he was doing odd jobs in order to help his mother keep the family in one piece.

Inspired by trade-unionist family members, Zuma signed up with the ANC two years later, and joined its armed wing, Umkhonto we Sizwe, in 1962. He was arrested the following year, along with forty-odd other young MK men, and was convicted of treason at just 21 years old. Zuma was sentenced to spend ten years – the rest of his twenties – on Robben Island together with the likes of Nelson Mandela and Walter Sisulu. His future path had been defined, and he would go on to play an important role in the struggle for liberation, fleeing to Swaziland in 1975 (where he first met Thabo Mbeki), being elected a member of the ANC's National Executive Committee in 1977 and being appointed Chief Representative of the ANC in Mozambique in 1984. He was forced out of that country in 1987, relocating to the ANC's headquarters in Lusaka, Zambia, where he played a crucial and defining role as head of the organisation's counterintelligence. As ANC spy-chief until the early 1990s, his was a position of considerable power, and he would have been privy to information that likely served him well in the years to come.

So this is the context that must be taken into account when the role of Jacob Zuma is considered in the recent and future political landscape of South Africa. Among all the controversy and embarrassment he has wrought on the nation, herein lies, if not the excuse, the explanation for much of it.

There can be little objective doubt that Jacob Zuma's lust for the presidency – though he always claimed he was simply following ANC wishes for him to assume the role – has been massively damaging to South Africa's institutions and to South African democracy. And it divided the nation like nothing has since 1994.

> "We have seen enough of this man to conclude that he considers himself untouchable; not by any sense of shame or contrition; not by the African National Congress's code of conduct; and certainly not by a big disease with a little name."
>
> – *Jacob Dlamini*

> "He is a spendthrift and scrounger who writes rubber cheques and forges sleazy relationships with crooked businessmen willing to bankroll his appetite for the good life he cannot afford."
>
> – *Drew Forrest*

There were certainly some speed humps along the way, most famously his on-off corruption trial, which revealed how an obsequious, oily little man by the name of Schabir Shaik had entered into a "mutually beneficial symbiosis" with him after his return from exile. Shaik was eventually convicted and sent to jail for, among other things, bribing Zuma *(see Shabir Shaik)*, and the corollary logic concluded that Zuma would follow suit for accepting these proven bribes. It was just one of many allegations against ANC politicians to do with the notorious arms deal – there remains a widely held belief that many more should have been, or should still be, charged *(see Joe Modise)* – but the facts were damning and incontrovertible in this case. Money had illegally changed hands; Zuma had sold out his country.

In relieving Zuma of his position as deputy president of South Africa shortly after the conclusion of the Shaik trial, Thabo Mbeki had this to say: "In the interest of the honourable Deputy President, the government, our young democratic system and our country, it would be best to release the honourable Jacob Zuma from his responsibilities as Deputy President of the republic and member of the cabinet." He was spot on; it *was* absolutely in the interest of South Africa to toss out a corrupt politician. But Mbeki was also deeply embroiled in the affair.

"I for one would not be able to hold my head high if a person with such supporters were to become my president, someone who did not think it necessary to apologise for engaging in casual sex without taking proper precautions in a country that is being devastated by this horrendous HIV/Aids pandemic. What sort of example would that be setting?"

– *Desmond Tutu*

"The rise of the movement to place in power Jacob Zuma – at best an incompetent, at worst a man who believes it is acceptable to take bribes – poses a grave risk to this country."

– *Ray Hartley*

Zuma was investigated by the Scorpions, and after a tortuous process that was drawn out over several years, consuming millions of rands' worth of taxpayer funds and endless column inches in the country's newspapers, charges against him were laid and dropped and laid and dropped, until it was finally judged that there had been too much political interference in the case by the Mbeki-led administration. As of 6 April 2009 – just weeks before the 2009 general election – Zuma was in the clear, not because he was innocent, but because his political arch-foe had been found out. The ultimate irony is that, had Mbeki and all those who lived in horror of a Zuma presidency allowed due process to take place, it's entirely likely that Zuma would currently be in Leeuwkop, not Tuynhuis.

And, really, he should be. This escape by technicality hangs around Zuma like a bad smell. Everyone – at home and abroad – now simply assumes the president is corrupt. And many of his actions, such as the disbanding of the Scorpions immediately after he assumed the ANC presidency at Polokwane, and the appointment of Menzi Simelane as director of the National Prosecuting Authority, seen by many as a manoeuvre that has catastrophically damaged the independence of the institution, have only served to reinforce this belief.

Corruption is, however, only half the problem. Zuma isn't only corrupt (as per the Shaik ruling); he is deeply unsophisticated while president of a country that has a highly sophisticated constitution.

In 2005 he was charged with rape and taken to court. The accusations turned out to be bunkum, with the trial quite likely cooked up by Zuma's enemies. The judge found that the sex was consensual and admonished the accuser for lying in her testimony. But the case exposed Zuma as reckless and disbelievingly ignorant about one of the gravest challenges to face this country: Aids. During the trial it was revealed that he had not worn a condom while having sex with the woman, whom he knew to be HIV-positive – this despite Zuma having chaired the South African National Aids Council. In testimony that would go on to be much maligned, and still haunts him today, he explained that he had showered afterwards to help avoid catching the virus.

"If a man cannot think sensibly when dealing with his basic urges, how can he be trusted with guiding the national economy, or managing the fundamentals of government responsibility?"

– Patricia de Lille

"Perhaps before engaging in such activity (sex with a woman who was not one of his wives), he should have checked first with an expert in the field, perhaps the former head of the Moral Regeneration Campaign. Oops, that's him."

– Sunday Independent editorial, April 2006

While the farcical shower comments dominated coverage of the trial, Zuma's archaic attitudes to women's rights also came to the fore. His accuser was half his age, the daughter of a (dead) friend and, as Zuma explained it, she had intimated her desire for sex by not wearing underwear. Later he had felt obliged to have unprotected sex because, as the *Mail & Guardian* scathingly paraphrased him, "it was against Zulu culture to leave a woman in a state of arousal". Even more damningly, Zuma refrained from censuring the thousands of vociferous supporters in attendance, many demanding vengeance on his accuser and bearing banners declaring "Burn the bitch". Rather, he played up to them, singing the struggle song *Umshini Wami* – with the line "bring me my machine gun" – at every opportunity. The damage to women's rights was inestimable and roundly condemned.

Isn't it still staggering, all these years later? This particular trial and all the rest: the corruption concerns; the homophobic slurs; the affairs; the many children –

22 now, apparently – from the many different wives and girlfriends. It is not hard to understand the fear and concern that Zuma struck into Mbeki and so many others. He was the stereotype, the African tinpot dictator with his AK-47 and his ridiculous sexual shenanigans and regular disregard for democratic institutions and norms.

"Mr Zuma, who is polygamous, has been married five times. He and his second wife, Nkosazana Dlamini-Zuma, are divorced. His third wife, Kate Mantsho-Zuma, committed suicide in 2000. He recently married his fifth wife, the 37-year-old Tobeka Madiba-Zuma. It has been reported that Mr Zuma recently fathered his 20th child, and will soon marry again. He is engaged to Gloria Bongi Ngema of Durban."
    – *New York Times official biography of Jacob Zuma as of June 2010*

"'An odious populist" … "A person of dubious morals, a demagogue and a rabble-rouser who spends most of his time eluding prosecution for corruption."
    – *André Brink*

And yet his rise to the top proved to be unstoppable. He had "uncorked the power of populism", as one journalist phrased it, and it took him all the way to the presidency. For all the damage he'd done as a moral example and as a political distraction in the years before, he now had to run the country. Luckily for him – and in many ways *because* of him – he had a much-maligned act to follow. Thabo Mbeki had wrought so much damage in his time that the ascent of Zuma was finally deemed acceptable by all, despite his evident lack of aptitude for the job.

Predictably, his private life remains a problem. In January 2010 Sono Khoza, daughter of Zuma's friend and soccer magnate Irvin Khoza, gave birth out of wedlock to his latest child. It was yet another embarrassment for the ANC to handle, especially in light of the party's quite sensible "One girlfriend, one boyfriend" campaign to curtail the spread of HIV and Aids. As Patricia de Lille put it, Zuma had been asking people "to do as I say and not as I do".

This, of course, is the hallmark of the big man. The rules do not apply to people like Zuma. He may have a fondness for getting young women pregnant, but when it's not his spawn he has said that their babies should be taken away and the girls forced to go to university to get degrees.

Of more concern, though, is Zuma's ability to actually perform as president, to get things done. It seems unlikely that he could do as much damage as Mbeki did, though we wouldn't want to talk too soon – it's certainly within the realms of possibility. Many of his appointees to important institutions, such as the NPA and Human Rights Commission, have undermined their independence, while the increasing frequency of "cadre deployment" to critical ministry and parastatal positions has catastrophic potential in the long run. Equally worrying are the proposed Protection of Information Bill and Media Appeals Tribunal that have arisen on his watch.

But the problem, after JZ's first year and a half in charge, is more that he hasn't actually done anything at all. The man may well be charming in the flesh but, after all that effort to get there, it's hard to understand why he wanted to become president in the first place. He's simply blown with the wind, appeasing here, placating there – and fiddling as the country burns. The Soccer World Cup was great, but the country drifts along aimlessly. Corruption is all but endemic, service delivery worsens, the poor get poorer and the vacuum of strong leadership creates space for the likes of Julius Malema to flourish. Zuma shows no sign of having a powerful agenda to improve the country or to root out corruption.

Indeed, the only agenda Jacob Zuma appears to worry about is Jacob Zuma. As long as JZ is getting the treatment as the big man, and getting the girls, he's happy. Who's running the country? Who knows?

But never fear. We'll be fine. We always are.

Bibliography

Books: • *Africa: A Biography Of The Continent* by John Reader (Alfred A Knopf, 1998) • *African Tears* by Cathy Buckle (Covos Day Books, 2001) • *Anatomy Of A Miracle* by Patty Waldmeir (Penguin Books, 1997) • *An Appetite For Power: A History Of The Conservative Party Since 1830* by John Ramsden (Harper Collins, 1998) • *The Bang-Bang Club* by Greg Marinovich and Joao Silva (Arrow Books, 2001) • *Blacks, Boers* by Francis Reginald Statham (General Books, 2009 – originally published 1881) • *The Boer War* by Thomas Pakenham (Avon, 1992) • *Captain In The Cauldron* by John Smit and Mike Greenaway (Highbury Safika Media, 2009) • *Commando* by Denys Reitz (Faber & Faber, 1943) • *Complete Kak! The Comprehensive Whinger's Guide To South Africa And The World* by Tim Richman and Grant Schreiber (Two Dogs, 2009) • *Diamonds, Gold And War* by Martin Meredith (Jonathan Ball Publishers, 2007) • *Into Africa: A Journey Through The Ancient Empires* by Marq de Villiers and Sheila Hirtle (Phoenix Giant, 1997) • *Jan Smuts: Man Of Courage And Vision* by Antony Lentin (Jonathan Ball Publishers, 2010) • *The Last Trek: A New Beginning* by FW de Klerk (Macmillan, 1998) • *Leon Schuster's Lekker Thick South African Joke Book* by Leon Schuster (Zebra, 1998) • *The Letters Of Anthony Trollope, Vol 1*, edited by N John Hall (Stanford University Press, 1983) • *Making The Rugby World: Race, Gender, Commerce*, edited by Timothy Chandler and John Nauright (Routleedge, 1999) • *New History Of South Africa* by Hermann Giliomee and Bernard Mbenga (Tafelberg, 2008) • *The Penguin Dictionary Of South African Quotations* by Jennifer Crwys-Williams (Penguin, 2008) • *A People's History Of Britain* by Rebecca Fraser (Pimlico, 2003) • *The Scramble For Africa* by Thomas Pakenham (Avon, 1992) • *South Africa's Brave New World* by RW Johnson (Penguin Books, 2010) • *The Washing Of The Spears* by Donald R Morris (Simon and Schuster, 1965) • *Wilfred Thesiger: The Life Of The Great Explorer* by Alexander Maitland (Harper Collins, 2006) **Film and audio:** *Infamous Assassinations: The Assassination Of Dr Hendrik Verwoerd*, Nugus/Martin Productions, 2007 • Much of the Anglo-Zulu War information was gleaned from the collected Zulu oral history as recounted by David Rattray. A tiny fraction of this is saved for posterity and is available for sale as a recording called *The Day Of The Dead Moon*, written and narrated by David Rattray. **Paper:** "Apartheid Mythology And Symbolism. Desegregated And Re-invented In The Service Of The New South Africa: The Covenant And The Battle Of Blood/Ncome River" by Anton Ehlers, published in *Alizés, Revue Angliciste De La Réunion*, no 24, 25-29 March 2003 **Websites:** www.abc.net.au • www.africancrisis. co.za • www.anc.org.za • www.arrivealive.co.za • www.bleacherreport.com • www.books. google.com • www.cricinfo.com • www.dailymail.co.uk • www.financialmail.co.za • www. gripen.com • www.iol.co.za • www.mg.co.za • www.mmegi.bw • www.news24.com • www. newyorker.com • www.nyt.com • www.politicsweb.co.za • www.sahistory.org.za • www. thedailymaverick.co.za • www.thisislondon.co.uk • www.time.com • www.timeslive.co.za • www.timesonline.co.uk • www.trutv.com • www.washingtonpost.com • www.whosewhosa. co.za • www.wikipedia.com • www.youtube.com